An Ethnoarchaeological Study of the Blacksmithing Technology
in Cebu Island, Philippines

T0352608

European University Studies

Europäische Hochschulschriften
Publications Universitaires Européennes

Series XXXVIII
Archaeology

Reihe XXXVIII   Série XXXVIII
Archäologie
Archéologie

Vol./Bd. 78

PETER LANG

Frankfurt am Main · Berlin · Bern · Bruxelles · New York · Oxford · Wien

Jocelyn B. Gerra

An Ethnoarchaeological Study of the Blacksmithing Technology in Cebu Island, Philippines

PETER LANG
Internationaler Verlag der Wissenschaften

Bibliographic Information published by the Deutsche Nationalbibliothek
The Deutsche Nationalbibliothek lists this publication in the Deutsche Nationalbibliografie; detailed bibliographic data is available in the internet at http://dnb.d-nb.de.

Zugl.: Hamburg, Univ., Diss., 2005

Cover Image:
Soil at the bottom of the anvil is either dug deeper
or filled with soil to adjust the proportion
between blacksmith or his assistant to the height
of the anvil (Jocelyn Gerra).

D 18
ISSN 0721-3530
ISBN 978-3-631-63110-2
© Peter Lang GmbH
Internationaler Verlag der Wissenschaften
Frankfurt am Main 2013
All rights reserved.

All parts of this publication are protected by copyright. Any utilisation outside the strict limits of the copyright law, without the permission of the publisher, is forbidden and liable to prosecution. This applies in particular to reproductions, translations, microfilming, and storage and processing in electronic retrieval systems.

www.peterlang.de

Contents

Foreword

This dissertation is an expanded study of my unpublished Master's Thesis done at the University of San Carlos, Cebu, Philippines. The integration of picture and text is the result of Mr. Lars Achenbach's computer skills. The text was edited by Ken Mast. I would like to thank my advisor, Prof. Dr. Helmut Ziegert for giving me the freedom to design this study. His critique is a great inspiration and his helping hand when the rough draft get going is a great relief.

Abstract

One goal of ethnoarcheological research is as an exercise, or method, is to explore how to see the varying ways in which the behavior of living people create archeological contexts, and leave deposits that mark the outcome of their special activities. This is not so much to see what a living site might look like were it to become an archeological site, but to help archaeologists predict what evidence these might become in any archeological site.

Mapped were the toolmaking facilities like the forge, hearth, bellows, equipment used for casting, grinding, handle/case making and so with the smithing residue, the exfoliation associated with each facility. Different structures and alterations on the ground such as hearths and other associated materials were also noted. During the field study, it was noted that the manufacture of slag-like residue is noted to be a normal side result of the blacksmithing process. This observation intrigued the researcher, for the physical appearance resembled slags found in the Lapu-lapu/Magallanes site in downtown Cebu City excavated in 1967. The researcher showed the sample to the Basak blacksmiths and they claimed that it was the product of blacksmithing and even has a local term for it – *tambacong*.

The prevalence of slag in the Philippine archeological sites is a fact that cannot be ignored. These artifacts are mentioned in almost all archeological reports and in the artifact inventory record of the National Museum of the Philippines. Given this fact, there is a need to strengthen the information on the context in which these slags are generated. Ethnoarcheological researches are still few and far between in the Philippines. So far, we do not know of published ethnoarcheological research that has been done on blacksmithing debris depositional patterns. This research was to begin an expansion of ethnoarcheological research in the Philippines, beginning with blacksmithing.

Since the purpose of ethnoarcheology is to examine from a contemporary materialistic point of view, the variable conditions/situations that an artifact can be produced to prevent inaccurate or sweeping conclusions, one slag-like sample and one slag sample was subjected to semi-quantitative analysis. The archeological slag was obtained from the archeological collection of the USC Museum.

Among the debris that are likely to enter and remain in the archeological record include such debris as heavy concentration of ash, burnt charcoal and *tambacong*/blacksmiths slag, the residues from grinding/polishing. The activities related to handle/case attachment which will give the soil matrix a dark color due to decay in inorganic material like wood. And finally the furnace will clearly show up together with its associated *tambacong* deposits on the furnace wall.

The results of both the Scanning and EDAX analysis suggests that the archeological sample could have had the same origin as that of the Basak sample. That means from the blacksmith's hearth and not that of the smelter.

Deutsche Fassung

Ein Ziel der Ethnoarchäologie als Methode ist es zu unterscheiden, wie unterschiedliches menschliches Verhalten zu archäologischen Fundzusammenhängen führt und Ablagerungen hinterläßt, die das Ergebnis von bestimmten Verhaltensweisen widerspiegeln. Es geht dabei nicht so sehr darum zu zeigen, wie ein Siedlungsplatz ausgesehen hat, als er zu archäologischen Stätte wurde, sondern vorherzusagen, welche Befunde in jeder archäologischen Fundstätte zu erwarten sind.

In die Analyse mit einbezogen wurden die Einrichtungen, für die Gerätherstellung und ihre Beziehung zueinander wie Schmiede, Herd, Geräte für die Luftzufuhr, Gussutensilien, Schleifvorrichtungen, Griff-/ Scheidenherstellung sowie Schmiederückstände und Abblättern von Rost. Unterschiedliche Strukturen und Änderungen auf dem Terrain, etwa Herde und andere dazugehörige Materialien, wurden ebenfalls aufgenommen. Während der Feldforschung wurde erkannt, dass schlackenähnliche Rückstände ein übliches Nebenprodukt im Schmiedeprozeß darstellen. Diese Beobachtung führte die Autorin zu ähnlich aussehenden

Schlacken, die auf einer Grabung 1967 in der Innenstadt von Cebu City (Philippinen) gefunden wurden. Die Schmiede von Basak (Stadtteil von Cebu City) erkannten in diesen Überresten ein Schmiedeerzeugnis und benannten es mit einem lokalen Namen: *tambacong*.

Die Häufigkeit von archäologischen Schlacken auf den Philippinen ist offenkundig. Diese Artefakte werden in beinahe allen archäologischen Darstellungen und in den Bestandslisten des National *Museums of the Philippines (Manila)* erwähnt. Aufgrund dieser Tatsachen ist ein Vertiefen der Kenntnisse über die Fundzusammenhänge nötig, die diese Schlacken hervorbrachten. Ethnoarchäologen sind auf den Philippinen äußerst dünn gesät. Bisher gibt es keine veröffentlichten ethnoarchäologischen Arbeiten, die sich mit der räumlichen Verteilung von Schmiederückständen im archäologischen Befund befassen. Die Autorin hofft, mit dieser Arbeit weitere ethnoarchäologische Forschungen auf den Philippinen anzustoßen, im vorliegenden Fall selbst beginnend mit dem Schmiedehandwerk.

Die Ethnoarchäologie nimmt ihre Untersuchung von einem zeitgenössisch-materialistischen Standpunkt vor. Ein Artefakt kann unterschiedliche Konditionen/Situationen hervorrufen. Deshalb wurden eine schlackenähnliche und eine Schlackenprobe der semiquantitativen Auswertung unterzogen. Die archäologische Schlacke wurde für die Analyse von der University of San Carlos Museum (Cebu City) zur Verfügung gestellt.

Unter den Ablagerungen, die wahrscheinlich Einzug in die archäologische Aufnahme halten, befinden sich starke Aschekonzentrationen, Holzkohle und *tambacong*/Eisenschlacke sowie Rückstände vom Schleifen und Polieren. Tätigkeiten, die im Zusammenhang mit der Griff- und Scheidenherstellung stehen, führen im Boden zur dunklen Verfärbung, die durch Zerfall von organischem Material wie Holz verursacht sind. Schließlich wird sich der Ofen zusammen mit den *tambacong*-Rückständen klar abzeichnen mit seinen Ofenmauern. Das Ergebnis des Scanning und der EDAX-Analyse deuten an, daß die archäologische Probe dieselbe Herkunft haben könnte wie die Basak-Probe; das bedeutet vom Schmiedeherd, nicht vom Schmiedetiegel.

(Translation by Lars Achenbach, Department of Archaeology, University of Hamburg, Germany, October 2005)

1. Introduction

1.1 The Problem

Material remains of past human activity has been of great interest to the archeologist. Through these remains one gets to have a view of the past life of a people long dead but its behavior lives through the artifacts that they have left behind. Artifacts are human-made or modified objects, may it be of stone, pottery, metal or wood. These provide archeologists crucial evidence of the way of life of a people, their adaptation process and the contexts that they have had.

The focus of this study is the technological exploitation of iron. Metals have been known to humankind for approximately 10,000 years. The first known metal were those in pure form – that means they were found lying on the ground.

The cultures of the Mesopotamians, Egyptians, Greeks, Romans, Indus Valley to name a few have already known gold, copper, silver, lead, tin, iron and mercury. Of these seven metals, iron came later, for the working on iron needs more specialized tools to form this glowing metal. Copper and gold for example can be hammered cold. Iron needs a higher temperature to release its impurities. This can be done by hammering as in smithing to squeeze out the impurity, with the use of sophisticated set of work tools to be able to manage the working of the metal.

Alan Cramb gives us an overview of the behavior of these metals[1];

"Gold is widely dispersed through the earth's crust and is found in two types of deposits: lode deposits, which are found in solid rock and are mined using conventional mining techniques, and placer deposits which are gravelly deposits found in stream beds and are the products of eroding lode deposits. Since gold is

---

1   Alan Cramb. A Short history of Metals. Department of Metal Science and Engineering. Carnegie Mellon University (http://neon.mems.cmu.edu, accessed on 2005.09.15).

found uncombined in nature, early goldsmiths would collect small nuggets of gold from stream beds etc., and then weld them together by hammering.

The symbol for copper is Cu and comes from the latin cuprum meaning from the island of Cyprus. Initially copper was chipped into small pieces from the main mass. The small pieces were hammered and ground in a manner similar to the techniques used for bones and stones. Malachite, a green friable stone, was the source of copper in the early smelters. Originally it was thought that the smelting of copper was by chance dropping of malachite into campfires. However, campfire temperatures are normally in the region of 600–650 C, whereas, 700–800 C is necessary for reduction. It is more probable that early copper smelting was discovered by ancient potters whose clay firing furnaces could reach temperatures of 1100–1200 C. Lead is not found free in nature but Galena (lead sulfide) was used as an eye paint by the ancient Egyptians. Galena has a very metallic looking appearance and was, therefore, likely to attract the attention of early metalworkers.

Silver is the most chemically active of the noble metals, is harder than gold but softer than copper. It ranks second in ductility and malleability to gold. Galena always contains a small amount of silver and it was found that if the lead was oxidized into a powdery ash a droplet of silver was left behind.

The first tin artifacts date back to 2000 B.C., however, it was not until 1800 B.C. that tin smelting became common in western Asia. Tin is found as vein tin or stream tin. The tin ore is stannic oxide and is generally found with quartz, feldspar or mica. The ore is a hard, heavy and inert substance and is generally found as outcroppings as softer impurities are washed away. The Romans referred to both tin and lead as plumbum where lead was plumbum nigrum and tin was plumbum candidum.

Mercury, also known as quicksilver, is the only metal which is liquid at room temperature. Although it can be found in its native state, it is more commonly found in such ores as calomel, livingstonite, corderite and its sulfide cinnabar.

Iron was available to the ancients in small amounts from meteors. Iron is rarely found in its native state the only known sources being Greenland where the iron occurs as nodules in basalt that erupted through beds of coal and two very rare nickel-iron alloys. Wrought iron was the first form of iron known to man. The product of reaction was a spongy mass of iron intermixed with slag. This was then reheated and hammered to expel the slag and then forged into the desired shape."

1.1.1 Rationale of the Study

The problem area which ethnoarcheologists have chosen to explore is, first, learning to see how patterned human cultural behavior in living, ethnographic contexts lays down or deposits evidences of that behavior, and, second, to see how these deposits from live activity can strengthen the archeologists' interpretations of deposits in archeological contexts (sites) by analogy. To do this, the archeologist starts with ethnographic research. The findings are then available for future archeological interpretation of data excavated in archeological sites. It may be, for example, that a number of different processes have resulted in highly similar deposits in different sites, but these processes are no longer visible. Ethnographic study of these varying processes among living people can observe the social context and behaviors that result in similar deposits. Thus, the archeologists need not be shackled in their interpretation by assuming a simple connection between one result and one type of behavior producing it.

Ethnoarcheological researches are still few and far between in the Philippines. So far, we do not know of published ethnoarcheological research that has been done on blacksmithing debris depositional patterns. This research was designed to begin an expansion of ethnoarcheological research in the Philippines, beginning with blacksmithing. While complete metallurgical processes beginning with smelting and concluding with the manual technology of processing iron into tools is seldom seen in full practice today, the later process – blacksmithing – is still available for observation in Cebu Island as well as in other parts of the Philippines. It should be noted however, that this local technology or trade is dying as a result of the influx of western and modern designed goods.

This study thus has selected a technological process for ethnographic attention, a process that is still observable in the culture of the researcher. Metallurgy has been of great importance to the evolution of human societies from prehistoric times. An ethnoarcheological study of it may further lead to the interpretation of important archeological sites in the Philippines that show evidence of metallurgy.

One goal of ethnoarcheological research is as an exercise, or practice, in learning how to see the varying ways in which the behavior of living people creates archeological contexts, and leaves deposits that mark the outcomes of their special activities. This is not so much to see what a living site might look like were it to become an archeological site, but to help archeologists predict what evidence these might become in any archeological site. Ethnoarcheology helps to provide archeologists with the interpretative skills to look at the effects certain causes might have had in prehistoric cultures based on an increased awareness of how they occur in various living context.

1.1.2 Statement of the Problem and Hypotheses

Within the problemarea of expanding and improving ethnoarcheological practice, the problem of the present thesis resolves itself into the following statement:

> *To determine how living human work activities (both as socially organized and individually expressed) that go into the technological processes of production in blacksmith shops in Basak, Cebu, produce archeologically relevant patterns of material culture in their specific work areas.*

To arrive at concrete facts to this statement, hypothetical formulation of best-guess possibilities is necessary for simplification and to guide the research. Hypotheses can be generated relating to directly observable archeological deposit indicators or exfoliation patterns, tool morphological variation and functional differences, and activity sites and patterns that can be differentiated according to primary and secondary activities. The hypotheses are as follows:

1. In the Cebuano blacksmithing shop, work processes of tool production form residues that are likely to be archeologically relevant.
2. Residue variations in the work flow of smithing activities can be distinguished.
3. Smithing activities will result in modifications of the work space floor that can serve as indices for those activities.

4. Primary activities (from metal cutting to the completion of smithing) and secondary activities (shaping and sharpening) lead to the formation of specific locations within the workshop that can be distinguished from each other.
5. Primary activities are located centrally in the workshop while secondary activities are located on the periphery.

The study aims to also explore the following:

Production Center

1. When was blacksmithing practiced in Cebu?
2. Where was it first practiced?
3. Was smelting also practiced?

Source and Origin:

1. If so, are there sources of iron ore in and around Cebu?
2. Could it have been imported from neighboring islands?
3. If not, could iron be one of the trade goods brought by the Chinese to the islands?

Production Distribution

1. For the local smith, were the products only for local use or was it also traded to other islands?

1.1.3 Significance of the Study

The study is designed to gain more insights and understanding of the formation process of blacksmithing in archeological sites. It has especially brought up the question on how one can tell the difference between slag from smelting obtained from archeological contexts and that of a slag-like deposit taken from the hearths of ethnographically documented blacksmith's workshops. The findings of this research will be of cautionary use to other archaeologists working in sites where metal working is encountered.

Secondly, the researcher aims to put to document a traditional technology before it is completely forgotten by the next generation. It is an indigenous technology that is loosing it significance in a fast-changing and highly western-influence society. These tools were actually part and parcel of everyday Philippine culture and a part of the adaptive mechanism of this society.

1.2 The Limits of the Research

The research will focus on blacksmith practices in the Island of Cebu. It is designed to gain more insights and understanding of the formation process of blacksmithing in archeological sites. It will focus on the question on how one can tell the difference between slag from smelting obtained from archeological contexts and that of a slag-like deposit taken from the hearths of ethnographically documented blacksmith's workshops. The findings of this research will be of cautionary use to other archaeologists working in sites where metal working is encountered.

The research area was in Carcar and in Basak, Cebu City. An economic and technical survey done by Leonidas Tan in Basak in 1966 reported a total of eighty (80) blacksmith workshops varying in manpower[2].Blacksmith shops are diminishing due to the presence of more lucrative cottage industries

As an ethnoarcheological study of blacksmithing the goal is to reconstruct the material remains of a blacksmith shop. One aim of ethnoarcheological research is – as an exercise or practice –, learning how to see the varying ways of the behavior of living people and that one creates archeological contexts, and leaves deposits that mark the outcomes of their special activities. This is not so much to see what a living site might look like were it to become an archeological site, but to help archaeologists predict what evidence these might become in any archeological site.

---

2   Leonidas Tan, "The Economics of Blacksmithing Industry in Basak, Cebu City 1969" (Cebu City: unpublished Master Thesis, University of San Carlos)

Ethnoarcheology helps to provide archaeologists with the interpretative skills to look at the effects certain causes might have had in prehistoric cultures based on an increased awareness of how they occur in various living context.

As a methodology, ethnoarcheology is seen as a way to prevent/caution archaeologists from reaching premature and inaccurate conclusions in this way, for events that create and give meaning to an artifact in a past setting take a different form from those that exist in societies contemporary with us. Methods are needed to justify better the inferences archaeologists make in interpreting their sites. The human organizations that give rise to specific human behaviors and to specific things need to be taken into account.

1.3 The History and Standard of Research

One can say that other than the discovery of fire, the invention of the first rudimentary tools, the practice of agriculture, the exploitation of metal has contributed significantly to the emergence of a complex, highly organized and socially differentiated society.

The study of the emergence of iron technology is very fascinating and a challenge to the archaeologists. This study will try to explore the extend of iron working technology and will focus on documenting the work process in blacksmithing and the residue that is deposits on the ground.

The emergence of an "Metal age" is still a much debatable issue although evidence suggest an evolutionary sequence from Bronze to Iron is present. Although this generalization must be taken with much caution. Research on iron technology in mainland Southeast Asia is far more comprehensive and there is a consensus among southeast Asian archeologists that iron was introduced from the mainland. The levels of the introduction of iron differ from place to place. The Southeast Asian neighbor of the Philippines, Thailand have made strides in the study of prehistoric metallurgy with the excavations in Ban Chiang.

Chen[3] wrote a comprehensive review of the history and emergence of iron technology in Northeast Asia, China, Southeast Asia citing the state of research. The study gives the reader a sweeping view of the state of iron technology research and the evidences that it might suggest. Going through this work one gets the impression that for the Philippines has lag so much behind in this subject.

In the Philippines it is widely believed that the "Iron age" began sometime between 500–200 BC. This is however based on a very fragmentary evidence of iron artifacts and the associated pottery recovered through archeological excavations.

Unlike the archaeology of many other closely related areas of the world, where chronology and typology of artifacts is fairly established, Philippine metallurgical studies is still at its infancy and thus very sketchy. Data available lacks a firm chronological, typological and regional ordering.

Solheim[4] has studied the ceramics classified by Beyer as belonging to the "Philippines Iron age", it was however not clear if there was really an iron age in the Philippines. In his book "Archeology of Central Philippines" believes that metal was not indigenous to the country but was brought in by the metal using Malays. He characterized the Iron age in the Philippines with smelting and forging of iron, manufacture of pottery, cloth weaving and manufacture of glass ornaments.

Hutterer[5] in Houses Build on Scattered Poles commented that trade between two societies to be functional and sustainable should have something in common with each other to exchange. That means that the trader comes with trade goods to trade with the local society and in return the trader or traders should be able to get some tradable good in return to the place of origin or that he can also trade with other society. Since geologically evidence does not speak of iron deposit that can be easily

---

3   K. Chen, Ancient Iron Technology of Taiwan.Ph.d Dissertation, Harvard University, Massachusetts.2000.

4   W.G. Solheim, The Archaeology of Central Philippines: A Study Chiefly of Iron Age and its Relatiotionships. Bureau of Printing Manila (1964).

5   K.L. Hutterer and William K. Macdonald,(eds). Houses Build on Scattered Poles: Prehistory and Ecology in Negros Oriental, Philippines. Cebu City, San Carlos University Press (1982) p. 8.

mined by the local population then the only means that the local population can have access to iron was through Chinese trade.

If a well developed metal technology had existed in the Philippine prehistory, this implies craft specialization, a relatively differentiated economy which can afford the energy expended in the extracting, processing and distribution metals and a trade network that brings together ores and fuels and disposes of the finished product.

Dizon[6] studied 75 objects from the Guthe-Michigan collection which was dated from the 10th to 15th Century. Twenty-eight are made of wrought iron, 23 of high carbon steel, 22 medium carbon and 2 of cast iron. His dissertation concluded that to date there has been no site found from which give evidence or suggest the presence of massive production on a large scale industry of iron in the Philippines. He further mentioned that so far the evidence suggest an iron- using society rather than iron producing. Ethnographic records has no account of any large scale iron production in the archipelago. Balunia[7] in her report on test excavations in Astillero site in Sorsogon mentioned that the site was engaged in iron and copper smelting.

1.3.1 Theoretical Background

A very selective and brief review follows of the thinking that led to the creation of ethnoarcheology, and an example of its application in the Philippines. In the period prior to about 1970, archaeologists were most likely to interpret the past of an archeological site by first making a thorough description of the site similar but a living society by social and cultural anthropologists. This method of interpretation was called "ethnographic analogy".

---

6   E.Z. Dizon. Iron Age in the Philippines? A Critical Examination. Ph.d Dissertation. University of Pennsylvannia. University Microfilm International. Ann Arbor (1988).

7   M.J. Balunia. "Preliminary Report on the Archeological Exploration and Test Excavations of the Astillero Site,Dancalan, Donsol,Sorsogon" National Museum of the Philippines (Typscript, 1995).

In the 1970s this approach came under increased attack. It was realized that archeological sites may be the result of totally different kinds of events and situations than are experienced by even present-day indigenes who are no longer believed to have been static with regard to social and cultural change. Therefore, it was recognized that ethnographic data generated from studies in present contexts, when used to interpret archeological materials, can lead to a misrepresentation of the past. In this method of breathing life into static, archeological remains, two things unfortunately happen.

(a) Archeologists do not link archeological records with the socio-cultural milieu of ancient peoples but with the milieu of their own day[8]; and

(b) Ethnographic and archeological artifacts are used to explain culture when in fact they must themselves be explained by the cultural context in which they are found. This is illustrated in Figure 1:

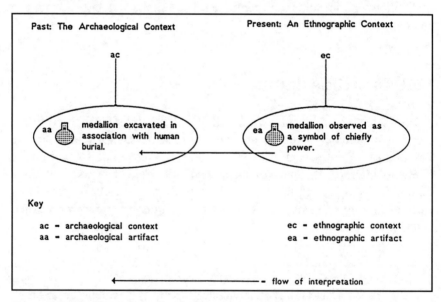

Figure 1: Mode of Explanation using Ethnographic Analogy

---

8   Lewis Binford, "Data, Relativism and Archeological Science", *Debating Archaeology* (California: New Academic Press, Inc. 1989), pp. 54–87.

To explain the meaning of the medallion[9] *aa* in Figure 1 within the archeological site *ac*, the archaeologist turns to ethnographic data from a living people at a similar level of technology in which a medallion is worn by a chief as a symbol of his political power. The archaeologist suggests that this archeological context is analogous and that the human burial with which a medallion was buried is that of a headman or chief. But the possibility arises that, in the prehistoric culture, the medallion was not so closely analogous to that, but rather, was a symbol of religious power. Further study of living societies might also find a culture where the pendant has religious significance.

In short, the relationship *aa – ac* may be erroneously interpreted as having been like the relationship *ec – ea*. The context *ac* is thought to have been understood. Thus, while *ea* is understood as a part of/from within its own ethnographic context, *aa* is used quite in reverse, to explicate its context *ac*. The artifact is used to explain culture, which is putting the cart before the horse. Also, the archeological artifact is not explained by its own milieu, but by that of a living ethnographic context. Furthermore, the process by which *aa* was created within *ac,* or for that matter, *ea* within *ec,* is ignored.

As a methodology, ethnoarcheology is seen as a way to prevent/ caution archaeologists from reaching premature and inaccurate conclusions in this way, for events that create and give meaning to an artifact in a past setting take a different form from those that exist in societies contemporary with us. Methods are needed to justify better the inferences which archeologists make in interpreting their sites. The human organizations that give rise to specific human behaviors and to specific things need to be taken into account.

The history of arguments for and against ethnographic analogy and leading to ethnoarcheology has been summarized by Orme. Much of the impetus toward ethnoarcheology came from Lewis Binford. As Orme wrote:

"Binford's approach to ethnographic analysis differs from that of the majority of prehistorians who start with an archeological problem and search the ethno-

---

9   Marcelino Maceda, "Preliminary Report on Selected Archeological Sites in Southern Leyte: A Case for Salvage Archaeology", *University Journal* Vol. 4 (1991), pp. 53–73.

graphic literature for possible solutions. What he does is to start with a facet of human cultural behavior and then study it from both archeological and ethnographic perspectives."

Orme says that, in this light, ethnographic analogy should be to "provoke a wide range of possible interpretations and to generate an awareness of the diversity of the human cultural response[10]."

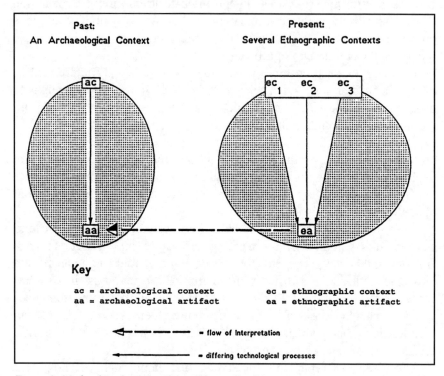

Figure 2: Mode of Explanation Using Ethnoarcheology

In ethnoarcheological research, the aim is to strengthen general knowledge of the relationships between artifacts, the processes by which they are formed, and the contexts in which they are made and used. This can be done in a living society. In a way, the old ethnographic analogy is turned on its head. The ethnographic context is looked at from an

10   Bryony Orme, "Twentieth-Century Prehistorians and the Idea of Ethnographic Parallels," *Man* (N.S.) 9, 199–212 (1974), pp. 210–211.

archaeologist's point of view, as if it were or might become an archeological site.

Debris-generating behavior is documented, first in one site, then in another site in differing but similar cultures. The generation of ethnographic data with the express purpose of strengthening archeological interpretation can improve bridging arguments, those arguments that bridge the chasm more plausibly from the ethnographic context to the archeological context (see Figure 2).

Only two noteworthy ethnoarcheological research projects have been carried out in the Philippines. Longacre has done a study of potters in Dangtalan, Kalinga, to investigate whether pottery making, which is there transmitted from generation to generation through nuclear families, resulted in the development of family styles or micro-developments through time[11].

Longacre studied indigenous systems of pottery classification, the steps in making pots, indigenous classifications of pottery soil, and the artifacts used in making pots, all to understand how people think about pots. A sample of different pottery types subjected to measurement and statistical analysis, confirmed the hypothesis that peoples' (nuclear families') pottery-making behavior and organization are subtly encoded in stylistic correlates of the pottery they make and use.

Mudar and de la Torre looked at one household in upland Negros Oriental to show how household members' behavioral activity may be reflected in the archeological record[12]. They found that in one important respect, behavior would not be so reflected. In the past, the Becino household accommodated a large family of nine children. Since the children married, many moved out into their own nuclear family households. This meant a drastic reduction in actually lived-in space. But this would not have been reflected in the house as an archeological site.

---

11   William Longacre, "Kalinga Pottery: An Ethnographic Study", *Past Studies in Honor of David Clarke.* I. Hodder, G. Isaac and N. Hammond (eds.), (Cambridge 1981). pp. 32–64.

12   Karen Mudar and Amalia de la Torre, "The Becino Site: An Exercise in Ethnoarcheology," K. Hutterer and W. Macdonald (eds.), *Houses Built on Scattered Poles: Prehistory and Ecology in Negros Oriental, Philippines,* pp. 117–146. University of San Carlos: Cebu City 1986).

All the behavioral activity of the reduced family could take place within the house without altering the ground plan in a way that would have been reflected archeologically.

In so far as studies on blacksmithing in the Philippines is concerned, there are only four studies which the researcher knows of at present. One is the unpublished master's thesis of Leonidas Tan which focuses on the economics of blacksmithing in Basak[13].

Mascunana of Silliman University, documents the making of fighting-cock spurs in Dumaguete City, Negros Oriental[14] and also made a family history chart for the respondents of his study which trace their origins and that of the technology to Basak. The third is a brief preliminary report on a survey of a blacksmith shop in the present study site[15].

Dizon in his study of the Philippine metal age made a suggestion relevant to this thesis where he identified a piece of iron in the Cortez site (circa 500 – B.C. – 500 A.D.) as "probably a slag" and recommended that it needed further analysis like EDAX, and others to determine whether it really is a "smelting" slag or a quartzite mineral[16]. In this recommend-dation, one tend to assumed that it was a slag from smelting and not from blacksmithing.

Hutterer in his report of archeological investigation in Cebu City also tends to see great amounts of slag found in his excavations at Lapu-Lapu and Magallanes Streets, as an indicator that a foundry center must have existed nearby, although he rejects the possibility that sherds to which slag was attached on their convex side to have been pieces of crucible.[17]

---

13 Leonidas Tan, *The Economics of Blacksmithing Industry in Basak, Cebu City* (unpublished Master's Thesis, University of San Carlos, 1969).

14 Rolando Mascuñana, "Blacksmiths and Gaffs in Dumaguete," *Philippine Quarterly of Culture and Society*, Vol. 17 (1989), pp. 175–201.

15 Amalia de la Torre and N. Tubalado-Cuevas, "A Preliminary Investigation of a Blacksmith's Workshop in Barangay Basak-Pardo, Cebu City" (Manila: Archaeology Record Section, National Museum of the Philippines 1990). (Typescript).

16 Eusebio A. Dizon, *The Metal Age in the Philippines: An Archaeometallurgical Investigation.* Anthropological Papers No. 12, National Museum, Manila (1983). See especially pages 18 and 55.

17 Karl Hutterer, *An Archeological Picture of a Pre-Spanish Cebuano Community.* San Carlos Publications No. 9 (1973), see pages 33–34, 56.

There is a tendency in the report to make no distinction between slags from blacksmithing and from smelting, and for slag to be identified with the smelting process and not the blacksmithing process. This is mentioned now, as the potential importance of making this distinction is an insight which is the result of the present preliminary investigation.

1.3.2 Conceptual Framework

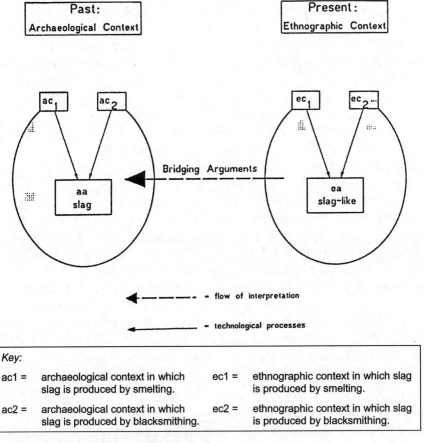

Figure 3: Conceptual Framework of the Study

To explicate the conceptual framework, which is shown in Figure 3, it will be helpful to preview an important finding here. This is the *discovery* that the manufacture of slag-like residue is noted to be a normal side result of the blacksmithing process. It is observed while doing an ethnoarcheological study of Basak blacksmith shops. This observation intrigued the researcher, for its physical appearance closely resembles slag found in the Lapu-lapu/Magallanes site in downtown Cebu City excavated in 1967[18]. In fact, when the researcher showed the sample to the Basak blacksmiths they claimed that it was the product of black-smithing. However, whenever slag has been discovered in archeological contexts in the Philippines, as suggested in the archeological report of the aforementioned site, it is usually or often attributed as evidence that smelting has taken place in the past. The questions arise, how do the processes by which slag produced in smelting differ from its production in smithing? Can physical examination discover any difference between the two types of slag? How can we know in an archeological context whether slag has been produced by smelting rather than by smithing?

According to the Merriam-Webster dictionary, slag is defined as being a product of smelting, refining or enameling and glazing. The definition given that is of relevance to this research. Slag is the dross of metal and specifically a product of smelting containing mostly as silicate, the substances not sought to be produced as matte or metal and having a lower specific gravity than the does the latter[19]. In short, a slag is a waste product. This definition not include products from blacksmithing, although the Cebuano *tambacong* as will be seen, contains large amounts of silicates. Therefore, for purposes of this work slag is defined as in Meriam and Webster, and slag-like material will be referred to the *tambacong* until a scientific basis can be found through various tests for claiming that they are the same or different. The question will be opened up by this thesis, through ethnoarcheology, is whether "slag" found in previous archeological sites is not really "slag-like" material produced in blacksmithing.

---

18 Hutterer, op. cit., p. 38.
19 Philip B. Grove and Merriam-Webster Editorial Staff, *Webster's Third New International Dictionary of English Language Unabridged* (Massachusset: Meriam-Webster Inc., 1981).

Aside from physical studies of slag produced by the different processes, the questions also demand an exploration of how slag is produced in different blacksmith shops and smelting sites in different cultures both ancient and modern (ec_1, ec_2, etc. in Figure 3). The basis for inferences that the slag found in Philippine sites was made by smelting must be improved. The comparison of ethnoarcheological studies of slag formation from technical processes in different cultures should improve the bridging arguments leading from the known, observable, systemic contexts to the unknown, static, archeological contexts. The discovery that slag is a by-product of blacksmithing in this ethnoarcheological study is a first step in this process, which is shown in the conceptual framework.

1.4 The Source of Data

The research was done in Basak and in Carcar, Cebu. One of the workshops cover in the study in Basak closed shop for it can not afford to maintain the overhead cost of production being the smallest among the three in terms of capital, production and manpower. Since the research is focussed on the activity of tool manufacturing and how these activities were reflected on the ground, these workshops were considered for in-depth study due to the following reasons:

1. These workshops have retained soil as the ground where work is done instead of a cement floor.
2. The workshops show diversity in terms of production output and capabilities.
3. These workshops are comfortably located a few meters from each other.
4. The study did not do an inventory of all blacksmith workshops for time and financial resources did not allow coverage of a larger area.

1.5 The Methods Involved

Ethnoarcheological research involves the combination of the methods of ethnography through participant observation and the basic archeological activity of map making of the site's boundaries and area. The major goal of this research was to establish the predictive patterns in the formation of smithing archeological sites. Thus, the approach presented here is to show how the researcher views the blacksmith workshop. As an observation strategy, the documentation process focused on two but related units of observation, namely; Behavioral Patterns of the Smithing Process and Directly Observable Archeological Deposits/Indicators.

The first observational unit looked into the technical aspects of smithing. It includes the documentation of the different steps in the manufacturing process – subdivided into process and activities making up the process. Under the first subdivision manufacturing process is further subdivided into classification of process whether primary or secondary and the corresponding equipment types used in the manufacturing process. Primary manufacturing refers to the tool manufacturing process from the cutting of metal into initial shape from the raw material until the shaping of a tool by smithing is achieved. Secondary manufacturing refers to the sharpening and shaping process of the blade of the tool, when the cutting edge of the blade is thinned out and the back of the tool made smooth. The structure/equipment type used is the sharpening machine. Another equipment/structure that is part of the secondary process is the hearth where the metals are heated. This is also used in the final process of tool manufacture – the finishing touches that require the use of heat in the tempering of metal and in the fitting of the handle.

The behavioral patterns of the smithing process create deposits on the ground that are directly observable and placed under the category of Directly Observable Archeological Deposits/Indicators. The smithing activity is the primary process of cutting, heating and hammering of metal into shape which deposits residual exfoliation of metal on the ground. For the aluminum and bronze, the indicators are fine metal particles for the former and burnt soil/earth, ashes and slag for the latter.

The central problem that this research dealt with were the predictive patterns indicating the processes of artifactual behavior as seen in a blacksmith workshop. First, the study covered the description of the arrangement of the facilities like the forge, hearth, bellows and furnace and the minor facilities such as those used in handle and case making, casting and grinding. To clearly understand the dynamics involved in the arrangement and set-up of the physical facilities, documentation was necessary of the frequency of construction and reconstruction processes and of the distinguishable characteristics left on the ground by them. Second, to tackle the behavioral, systematic aspect of the artifactual formation pattern of the entire blacksmithing activity, it was important to isolate the debris-generating activities as the artifact moves from one facility to the next.

Data gathering was divided into two phases: Technical Recording Procedures for Physical Facilities and Deposits, and Information Gathering from Blacksmith Workshop Personnel. These are discussed in more detail in the next page.

Technical Recording Procedures for Physical Facilities and Deposits. The first step in the recording process was the mapping of the general lay-out of the workshop. It included the inventory of different black-smithing facilities (those that are necessary for the making of tools) and the secondary facilities (those that constitute finishing up the tool, i.e. sharpening). The corresponding smithing residue, the exfoliation generated by each facility, will be developed as a flow-through analysis on the maps. Also included were the different structures and alterations on the ground such as hearths and other associated materials.

Mapping was the process of drawing a representation usually on a flat surface showing the area one wanted to represent, indicating the nature and relative position and size according to a chosen scale or projection of selected features or details.

A datum point for the site had to be established first to serve as the basis for all measurements of the site. The instruments used in mapping were: plane table, alidade, plumb bob, meter rods and tape measure.

1. *Plane Table.* This is a flat board where drawing is fastened for the plotting of the points measured. The table is mounted on a tripod and clamped in place. Once anchored, the table must be checked to see that it is parallel to the ground by using a line level.

2. *Plumb Bob.* A cylindrical metal piece with a pointed tip at the posterior end is used to transfer a point of a higher elevation to a point of lower elevation and vice versa. It also aids in transferring the vertical line of the datum point marked on the ground to the map. The bob is attached with a string and suspended from a clamp with a pointer on the map. The pointed tip of the bob should hit the center of the datum point that corresponds to the pointer.

3. *Alidade.* This instrument consists of a telescope with stadia hairs and a vertical arc for the measurement of vertical angles. This is affixed to the top of the plane table. Through the telescope of the alidade the surveyor locates the direction of the line to be drawn onto the map.

   The advantage of using the combination of alidade and plane table is that a site map can be drawn directly. Errors can also be corrected immediately while still in the field.

4. *Meter Rods.* The rod is a piece of fiberglass used in sighting points. It has a diameter of one (1) centimeter. It is equally and alternately divided into one-meter intervals of red or black and white. It usually has a length of two to three meters.

   The rod is held at a point and balanced in a vertical position so that the surveying person peering in through the alidade can visually assess the position of a point. The correct point is located when the vertical stadia hairs hit the center of the rod. Distance from the datum point to the rod is taken using a measuring tape.

   Other than the basic archeological equipment, a camera and Scanning Electronic Microscope (SEM) are included. The SEM was useful in the later part of the research to determine the physical structure of slag.

5. *Camera.* A 35 mm camera was used for the photographic documenttation of the blacksmithing process. A 35 mm Kodak Ektachrome 100 ASA slide film was used.

6. *Scanning Electron Microscope.* The Scanning Electron Microscope (SEM), Cambridge Stereoscan 180 used at an accelerating voltage of 8.20 KV (kilovolts), can magnify small-sized features of the surface of a sample (slag) for identification that goes beyond the limits of resolution of a light microscope. The SEM works with photographic tubes. Pictures from the magnified surface can also be made into plates and prints.

For the purpose of comparison of slag physical properties and differences, two general categories of samples (archeological and ethnographic) were examined under SEM. The samples were prepared for SEM by soaking in H_2O_2 (Hydrogen Peroxide) to remove the adherent clay from the slag samples. The specimens were rinsed in water and air-dried before spatter-coated with a few-micron-thick layer of gold-palladium in a vacuum evaporator. Samples were analyzed at the Institute for Geology-Paleontology, University of Hamburg, Germany.

Aside from the above technical documentation of the tool making processes, the researcher visited the workshops daily within the fieldwork period and noted down in the field notebook the different tool making activities of blacksmiths and other workshop facilities. This allowed the researcher to note which activities were responsible for the deposition of which residues.

It helped the researcher to distinguish the different activities and types of artifacts and the archeologically relevant patterning generated per activity. Photographic documentation of the different stages of tool manufacture was also done. Through the data gathered above, a model of residue patterns had been formulated and connected to the smithing process itself. These patterned relationships are the foundation of the archeological bridging arguments.

2. Landscape, Environment and its People

Adaptation is a key concept used in Cultural Anthropology to explain the adjustments and response of people to the environment they live in. It refers to the ability of a living system – organisms, populations and/or communities, in an ecological context – to regain stability under conditions of environmental change[20].

A glimpse of the map of Philippines shows an archipelagic country. In fact this is considered to be the largest archipelagic country in the world. It has about 7,100 Islands spread over 30 million hectares of land. The size would be about that of the former West Germany before the reunification in 1989. As an archipelago sitting on a very active Pacific tectonic plate, it has about two million kilometres of sea and has its share of very active volcanoes. It is bounded to the north and West by the South China Sea, the Celebes Sea to the south and on the east by the Pacific Ocean. It has three major group of Islands: Luzon, Visayas and Mindanao. Of the three major group of islands Visayas is the smallest of the three in terms of land area. The Visayas group of islands is geographically situated in Central Philippines and comprise the islands of Cebu, Bohol, Leyte, Masbate, Negros, Panay, Samar.

2.1 The Geology

The Visayan group of islands sits on the Visayan Basin. It is one of the largest basins in a tectonically active archipelago. The basement of the

---

20   E.S. Miller and C.A.Weitz, Introduction to Anthropology.(Englewood Cliffs, New Jersey: Prentice-Hall, Inc., 1979) p.470

Visayan Basin is comprised mainly of Cretaceous volcanic flows and intrusives and folded Cretaceous sediments.[21]

The uplifting and tilting of Cebu as a result of geological activity over time has resulted to a differentiated topography of the island. The central part of Cebu Island has very steep mountain range running in a North-South direction reaching up to 1,000 meters from sea level. As one goes southward the margin of land between the coast and the mountain is narrow. It is in the northward direction that one can find large alluvial land. The coastal part as well as a large part of the northern sector is dominated by the Carcar limestone formation which is a very porous, coralline limestone. The Carcar Limestone based on its topographic position indicates a major uplift of the island since the Pleistocene[22]. In geological time this is considered as the as the most recent formation. The oldest dated sediment in Cebu is the Tuburan Limestone of the Early Cretaceous[23].

The geological information[24] at hand will show that although Cebu has some ore resources such as Copper, Gold, Silver and Iron, these can only be harnessed with modern mining technology. This data has also a big impact on the livelihood of the people. One can therefore infer that since there is a lack of arable land and that the soil cover has the tendency to erode this makes the environment of Cebu very fragile. That means that the population has to adapt their livelihood to the limitations of the environment.

---

21   J. Foronda. Sequence Stratigraphy of an Oligocene-Miocene mixed Siliclastic Carbonate System, Visayan Basin, Central Cebu.Phils. (Bonn: Holos 1994)
22   H. Porth, C. Müller and C.H. von Daniels. "The Sedimentary History of the Visayan Basin, Philippines", Geol. Jb. Band 70 (1989) p.52.
23   Gramann in H. Porth et. al. p.36
24   P.C. Momongan. "Mineral Resources of Cebu Province and their Industrial Uses" (Typscript) Department of Environment and Natural Resources, Region 7, Mandaue, Philippines (December 1992)

2.2 The People

In 1521, a small fleet arrive at the coast of Cebu headed by Ferdinand Magellan, a Portuguese sailor who offered his services to the King of Spain, King Phillip II. This is where the Philippines got its name given by Magellan in honour of the king of Spain. His was welcomed to the shorts of Cebu by Humabon, the local chief of the barangay or community in what is today Cebu City. It must have been a warm welcome because Magellan was even allowed to plant the first Cross ever to stand on this side of the Pacific, sowing the seeds of Christianity and marked the start of Spanish colonization in the Philippines which was to last for 400 years.

Magellan wanted to extend his contact to the chief Lapu-lapu of Mactan, a neighboring island of Cebu, separated by a narrow strait. History records present that these two chiefs were in a feud so that the visit of Magellan was met with hostility and great resistance by the local people. In a battle on the shores of Mactan, Magellan was killed and this forced the retreat of the crew back to their ship.

The colonization of the Cebu and the rest of what is today the Philippines has also herald the introduction of written history. Documents on the history of the Philippines starting in the 16th century are mostly written by the clergy.

The Alzina documents[25] describe the native population as heavyset, huskier and taller than the natives of Luzon. He noted down that those living near the coast have a darker skin than those living in the interior part. Men and women both wear earrings and those in the affluent classes wear plenty of gold. Even the teeth was adorn with gold. This will give us an idea that social stratification was in place and a defined social class structure was in place. The document also presents the reader a people which took great care in hygiene. Alcina observed that houses were built along the coast and that the entire plain back to the mountains was dotted with houses but not arranged in any particular manner.

---

25   Alzina in J. Kobak, OFM. "Alzina's Historia de las Islas e Indios de Bisayas ..1668" Leyte-Samar Studies.Vol. III. No. 1 (1969).

2.3 Economy

Since the islands are separated by bodies of water, small planked-built boats[26] – locally called *banca, baroto* is the natual means of transportation. This supports the observation of Alzina that the local population lived along the coastal area or where navigable body of water was available. It could be inferred that these communities were also engaged in fishing, shell collecting to augment the resources that they get from farming and collecting wild fruits from the forest.

Bruce Fenner in his book[27] wrote based on the accounts of various 16th century documents showed a moderately sized, busy port, where trade with China, other parts of Southeast Asia as well as a thriving inland trade. This may be due to the fact that Cebu is centrally located for the other neighboring islands to come by boat. The port is also well-sheltered from tropical storms making it possible for boats to come and go even in the typhoon season. The good traded by the Chinese include porcelain, gold, slave and food supplies like rice, millet, sugar cane, palm wine (local name, *tuba*) local fruits as well as pigs raised by the Cebuanos. It could be inferred that through the Chinese the local "pandays"-blacksmiths, also a term used for carpenters- got hold of iron that they smithed to different kinds of tools.

Present-day Cebu's economy has not departed so much from it being a center of commerce in the Visayas as well as the introduction of other modern industries and crafts.

---

26   W.H. Scott. Cracks in the Parchment Curtain another Essays in Philippine History. (Quezon City, 1985).

27   B. Fenner. Cebu Under the Spanish Flag,1521–1896: An Economic-Social History. University of San Carlos Publications. (Cebu, 1985).

3. An Ethnoarcheology of Blacksmith's Shop

3.1 The Catalogue: Description of Blacksmith's Shop

This chapter documents how a blacksmith shop is structured physically in relation to the type of work that is needed. There is a long description of the lay-out plan and the equipment used in the production of tools. A unique indigenous (folk) health belief is discussed in relation to the description of the water trough.

In the description of the specific equipment, the ethnoarcheologically significant residues associated with each as a result of smithing activity have been described and located. Related to the previous statement, this chapter also included a description of the frequency of the maintenance of equipment since this activity has also a significant contribution to the debris generated in the blacksmithing activity.

Two maps, namely that of Silva Blacksmith Shop and that of Molo Abarquez Garden Tools Supply, are included to orient the reader to the lay-out plan of a typical blacksmith workshop in Cebu. A description of structure and equipment needed in the processing of tools follows including the frequency of maintenance of equipment. By elucidating each of these, the specific function and location in the workshop can be shown.

The structure of the workshop can be defined as the arrangements of its equipment. A description on the frequency of the maintenance of these equipments is also given special attention for this activity was seen to have significant contributions to the archaeological record.

The smithing workshop is a beehive of activity. It is necessary that the equipment be within easy reach of the workers, but at the same time, the workshop should be wide enough for ease of movement and good ventilation. In the workshops studied this is achieved by housing all the primary and secondary equipment in one shed.

The working sheds of the shops studied have galvanized iron roofing approximately five (5) meters high with no enclosing walls. In lieu of a proper wall, old galvanized sheets are used to block the sparks from neighbor's wood or bamboo fence, or the wall of a house that stands beside the workshop. This precaution is made due to the high population density in this area where houses are closely constructed to each other.

This is typical for Basak because over the years being located along the South Expressway of Cebu, the population grown into a proportion that there is a great demand for housing for particularly the migrant workers of Cebu City. Due to this "boom", landowners in Basak and surrounding areas rented their land to houseowners, build apartments, and/or constructed new houses to have the possibility renting out rooms or beds. As a consequence Basak became thickly populated that one can hear what the neighbors are talking. So that during the fieldwork it would be interesting to note that as researcher one gets to have an intimate view of the lives of those living near the blacksmith shop. In the process of interaction, it is very difficult at times for them to understand why one would waste time to study a technology which is "kara-an" –meaning old and traditional.

In contrast, the Carcar blacksmith shop is located at the edge of field and away from the houses of the local population. The shed has a high roof and the sides are either loosely covered with used small sheets of plywood that are not suitable for construction or provisional fenced with bamboo.

The shed structure is most suitable to the nature of smithing activities, which are hot and dusty. The absence of walls allow the movement of people in the workshop to be unrestricted. Air can flow and circulate freely, cooling the workshop workers, since the roofs are high. The ashes that blow from the hearth can not disturb or suffocate the workers since they are not trapped in the workshop.

The space occupied by the workshop is proportionate to the bulk of jobs done. Comparatively speaking, Silva's Hunting Knife Shop has the largest space, Mulo Abarquez Garden Tools Supply the smallest. The Basak workshops are located along Cebu's South Expressway, a strategic place for selling the products while that of Carcar is slightly on the interior part of town but middlemen and merchants come to pick up the products.

3.2 Description of Study Sites

Silva's Hunting Knife Shop
The shop is located beside the house of the owner but away from the road, the entrance of this establishment is on the West side of the workshop and used for exercising fighting cocks whose chicken coops can be seen right on the entrance. To the left is a pile of guava wood (*Psidium guajava*) that is exclusively used for bolo handles. Beside the pile is a workspace for handle and case makers.

Within this workspace stands a portable wooden bench and wood blocks to anchor the wood when a handle or case is carved. Portability of these structures allows the workers to move anywhere within the designated area to seek shade from the intense midday sun, shelter from the rain, since they are on the edge of the covered area, or to seek a cooler breeze during humid days. The space for the handle and case makers is also shared with two stationary stands for a grinding machine. The grinding machine and the table for wood boring are under the roof and are not portable.

A passage through the main shed is from the edge of the bellows nearest the entrance up to the intersecting water canals that mark the northern boundary of the workshop. Dividing this passageway is a work table where vise grips are mounted and where hunting knife handles are attached and manual grinding is done.

The three bellows are located in the southern section. Since much fuel is needed during production, charcoal is stocked near each bellows or on its own platform made of clay and connected to the hearth for easier access. Charcoal is also stocked near the furnaces where aluminum or bronze is melted. See Figure 4a + 4b below.

In terms of upkeep, the workshop is swept every other day and water is sprinkled after workshop is swept to keep the dust under control. Sprinkling of water is also done when there is much production and much ash is deposited/accumulated that even a slight wind creates a very dusty workplace. This is done also because this workshop doubles as a sleeping area for the stay-in workers.

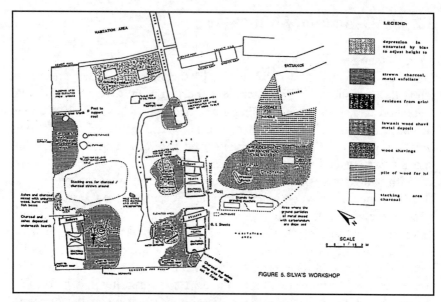

Figure 4a: Map of Silva Shop, Basak, Cebu

Figure 4b. A blacksmith worshop and store along the South Road, Basak, Cebu City

Mulo Abarquez Garden Tools Supply

This workshop is right in the front yard of the owner also on the South Expressway (see Figure 5 below).

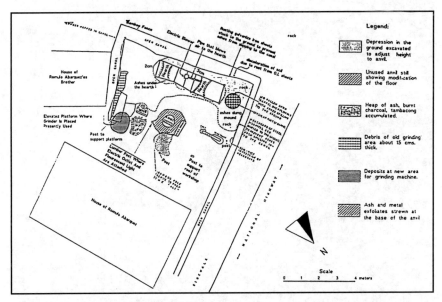

Figure 5: Map of the Abarquez Workshop, Basak Cebu

Between his house and shop is a passageway for people who live "inside" the neighborhood, the bellows and hearth are placed away from this trail and from people. The anvil is built on the opposite side. There is an extra anvil with a tree trunk for one of its posts but it is used only for shaping large metal pieces that the shop is occasionally commissioned to do.

One former polishing/grinding section is toward the southeast section of the workshop. One can still see the thick residue of fine carborundum particles and metal accumulated on the ground with a thickness of between 5–8 centimeters from ground build a surface (Figure 6). Mulo Abarquez stopped using this polishing/grinding area in 1988 when his brother decided to build a so close to the facility. The present location of electric grinder is now a small enclosed shed attached to the porch of the house. The floor of this grinding/polishing area is cemented and cleaned of shaving every other day. This shed also doubles as a storage for raw materials finished products.

Figure 6. A thick residue of fine carborundum particles and metal accumulated on the ground with a thickness of between 5–8 centimeters from ground

Carcar Blacksmith Shop

The Dapdap, Carcar blacksmith shop was included in the study so see if there was any difference in the structure of the workshop by the fact that is located in a small town and much open space to build the workshop. Based on the information gather from the blacksmiths in Basak, the blacksmiths in Dapdap, Carcar learned their craft in Basak. As a matter of fact up to the present the blacksmiths of Dapdap, Carcar come and work in Basak on demand or when they are in town and would like to earn a few pesos (Figure 7).

Figure 7. A blacksmith in front of his blacksmith shop in Dapdap, Carcar

3.3 Types of Equipment and Work Areas

It was observed that in the workshops, that the forge, which has the primary equipment, is located in the central section of the workshop while equipment used for secondary processes are placed on the periphery. In the following pages of this chapter, the different physical structures are described together with their functions.

Primary equipment is used in the production of the tool prototype or general shape and in further refinement of the tool's shape by polishing. Classified as primary are the forge, hearth, bellows, anvil, water trough and grinding and polishing machines.

Secondary structure/equipment is in the fitting of the handle and case (which are optional) and in tempering. Considered as secondary are the furnace for molding of metal handles, the hearth, and the handle and case makers' structure/equipment.

3.3.1 Primary Structures and Equipment: The Forge. (Figure 8)

Figure 8. The Blacksmith, his assistants and the forge

The forge is a place where metal is annealed. Annealing is a process where metal is heated and hammered into shape. Forging is a way of shaping metal by first heating and then hammering and pressing into shape. It improves the quality of metal, and refines its grain structure to be remarkably free of concealed or internal defects and therefore to have great strength and toughness[28].

---

28   John L. Feirer. *General Metals*. Third Edition (New York: McGraw-Hill, 1983), pp. 23.

The forge is considered the heart of the smithing process[29]. It comprises the hearth, bellows, charcoal container, anvil and water trough. The forge, together with the grinding machine, space for making the handle, and furnace for molding, are often all housed in one working shed especially in large scale production workshops.

1. The Hearth

The hearth is the place where metal is heated. It is actually a trough between two curvilinear clay mounds which function to concentrate heat in the trough (Figure 9). Large pebbles or broken hollow blocks serve as foundation for the walls of the hearth. It is covered with fine sandy clay which has been mixed with water and smoothed over the mound shapes. Between the two curvilinear mounds is a narrow, flat space where the charcoal is deposited to fuel and generate heat for metal to be worked.

Figure 9. The hearth which is actually a trough between two curvilinear clays mounds

---

29   Tan., op. cit., pg. 74. 73.

Figure 10. Detailed of hearth trough. The tuyere *showing an accumulation of molten metal and clay*

The size of hearth space used varies according to type of tool customarily worked. For hand tools (bolos, weeder, scissors, etc.) the opening is within the range of 20–25 centimeters. In a small workshop near the two workshops discussed here, the hearth is larger by three (3) times the size of these hand tool hearths since the owner specializes in tempering large tools like iron pipes used in digging artesian wells whose tubes have a length of one meter or more.

Near the bottom and center of one side of the hearth, more often observed along the left side of the blacksmith as he faces the hearth, there is a two (2) centimeter radius hole. It is about three centimeters from the base. This hole is the outlet of air blasts from the bellows known in English as the *tuyere* (Figure 10). To the right of the hearth is a flat surface also covered with clay or galvanized iron sheets and used as a charcoal container (Figure 11). Deposited charcoal from the sack beside the hearth makes the task of continuous refueling of the fire convenient and easy (Figure 12). A small shovel is used to scoop the charcoal in and out aided by a fire hook; the fire hook is also used to stoke the fire (Figure 13).

Figure 11. A flat surface to the right covered with galvanized iron or clay used as charcoal container

Figure 12. A sack of charcoal beside the hearth for easier access to refuel

Figure 13. Fire hook and small shovel used to scoop the charcoal and stoke fire

The blacksmith fire is small and concentrated in the middle part of the hearth where the bellows hole or *tuyeres* becomes very hot (Figure 14). The interior walls around this part and directly opposite thicken due to the accumulation of molten metal residue and molten clay from the charcoal and the hearth (Figure 15). The indigenous (Cebuano) terminology for this residue is *tambacong* – a slag-like material.

2. The Bellows (Figure 16)
Situated to the left of the hearth and connected to it by a lead pipe coming to the *tuyeres* perpendicular to the hearth is the bellows which provides strong blasts of air necessary to start a fire and maintain heat in the hearth. In Basak, blacksmiths are using two versions of the bellows – the wooden manually operated Malayan bellows which is traditional, (Figure 17 a–d) and the electric blower, a modern innovation (Figure 18).

Figure 14. Fire for smithing is small and concentrated in the middle part of the hearth

Figure 15. Detail thickening interior walls of hearth after a day's smithing

Figure 16. A wooden manually operated Malayan bellows

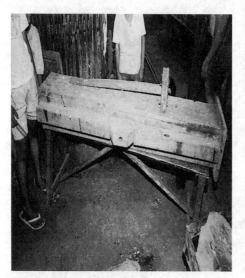

Figure 17a & b. Wooden bellows and piston-rod responsible for regulation of air to the hearth

Figure 17c. Detail of square end of plunger where duck feathers are attached

Figure 17d. Detail of air-hole where air from bellows pass to the hearth

Figure 18. Electric bellows, a modern adaptation

The wooden walls of bellows traditionally used by the blacksmiths of Basak are constructed out of thick slabs of 2.5 centimeters thickness. The bellows is rectangular in shape with an average length of one meter and twenty centimeters (120 cm) and a width of thirty centimeters (30 cm). The body is totally sealed except for two holes in front into one of which the piston-rod is inserted or fitted into. The piston-rod is responsible for the regulation of air in the chamber. It is operated with a thrusting and pulling motion so that the air chamber is made to expand to draw air through one valve and contract to expel air through another valve that leads to the *tuyere*. Leonidas Tan in his thesis "The Economics of the Blacksmithing Industry in Basak, Cebu City" accurately described how the bellows works. Thus, Tan wrote:

> *"When the wooden piston is pulled out, the air is admitted into the bellows by a small opening called valve #1 which is at the farther end of the bellows. At the same time, valve no. 2, which is at the front of the bellows, closes and acts as a plunger. During the operation, the trapped air is formed out into a hollow box forcing the air against the piston through the tuyere or air-hole to the fire pot. A 'feather socket' which is connected to the end of the wooden piston helps in*

compressing the air through the chambers in the bellows box. The width of the feather socket is just enough to tightly fit the inside wall of the chamber and make efficient the sucking in and forcing out of air"[30].

This box-type bellows evolved from the use of hollowed-out mentioned that his logs used during the Spanish period, according to one respondent. This respondent further stated that his grandfather used one in Carcar some years back.

A modification is the use of the electric blower. A small set of propellers encased in metal blows air through a nozzle to a pipe that exits into the hearth wall. The propellers are driven by electricity. Once the fire is bluish and embers are glowing, the machine is unplugged from the electric outlet. These are the same blowers that are used by foundry shop.

3. The Anvil

The anvil is where heated metal is to be made into a tool is placed for cutting and hammering into shape. It is often a thick slab of iron either circular or quadrangular in cross section. It is raised from the ground by pieces of log to about 45 centimeters (Figure 19a). The anvil is anchored well on top of the log with pieces of cut metal nailed to the sides of the log. In some instances, the shape of the anvil is carved into the log for better anchorage. In workshop B, the anvil is anchored by resting on one-half of a metal barrel filled with soil (Figure 19b).

At the base of the anvil a small piece of plywood or a piece of plain galvanized iron scrap is propped up by one or two pieces of lumber or bamboo to serve as a protection for the legs of the blacksmith and his assistant from the heated metal that exfoliates and drops to the bottom of the anvil in the course of shaping the tools (*Figure 20*).

The elevation of the anvil is often proportionate to the height of the blacksmith and his assistant. This proportion is strictly important to prevent or minimize back strain. In instances where the anvil is lower than the users, the soil at the bottom of the anvil where the workers stand is scraped or dug to a depth that provides a comfortable standing height (Figure 21). The opposite may be done when the user is lower than the anvil: the foot space is filled with soil or sometimes an elevated wooden

---

30   Tan., op. cit., p. 76.

Figure 19a. Circular iron slab used as anvil

Figure 19b. Another version of an anvil. A quadrangular iron slab anchored with clay flooring in a barrel

56

Figure 20. A lawanit piece used to protect the lower extremities of blacksmith and assistant from heated metal exfoliates

Figure 21. Soil at the bottom of the anvil is either dug deeper or filled with soil to adjust the proportion between blacksmith or his assistant to the height of the anvil

platform is used. The former arrangement is favored over the latter for it is more stable. Given such activity, modification of soil by filling and scooping are common in blacksmith workshops. The exceptions to this pattern in those workshops are where floors are cemented or where the same team (blacksmith and his assistant) work permanently together.

Below the anvil where the support posts are implanted and on the ground surrounding the anvil, one can find considerable metal exfoliation that has accumulated over time, forming a little hump. Mixed with it are some pieces of metal residue from the initial cutting and trimming of metal to the predetermined shapes. More often small (three centimeters in length or less) residue is found mixed with exfoliated metal for the larger pieces are collected at the end of the day to be sold later to the scrap metal dealer for recycling.

4. The Water Trough. (Figure 22)
Water is needed by the blacksmith to cool down heated metal and also for tempering of tools. The water trough, strategically placed beside the anvil, is elevated to an approximate height of the anvil. It is as long as necessary to dip a bolo blade into it. The water trough materials range from an aluminum recycled sink with holes patched with cement to a large tin can cut lengthwise, or a wooden basin. The water is changed everyday before work starts more often by the blacksmith's assistant. There is a folk belief attached to the water used in blacksmithing. Often at sunset, when all work ceases for the day, one can see blacksmith workshop personnel washing their faces and extremities with the used water. They believe that washing the day's grime off with this still, warm water can prevent *pasmo sa kusog*, an ailment that is characterized by a shaking of the whole body in extreme cases, or in a mild form just the arms or legs. It is widely agreed to be caused by the exposure of the tired and heated body while working in fire to the cool water in washing the day's dirt. To prevent this one must let the body rest overnight and take a bath early the next day. If washing beforehand cannot be avoided, then the warm water of the trough can be used as this is nearer to body temperature than water from an artesian well.

Figure 22. Water trough is strategically placed near the anvil to cool down heated metal

Some variations to the arrangement of the primary category were noted by the researcher in the blacksmith workshop of Romulo Abarquez and the shop nearby that belonged to his cousin.

In the workshop of Romulo Abarquez, the anvil and water trough is placed one and a half meters opposite and parallel to the hearth. In effect the blacksmith makes a 180 degree turn from the hearth to the anvil and vice versa. The water trough is placed to the left of the blacksmith and perpendicular to the anvil. With the blacksmith's assistant facing the anvil (his back to the hearth), opposite is where the blacksmith assistant stands. To the left of the blacksmith's assistant is a lumber post with an outlet and plug of the electric blower which he controls.

A variation to this arrangement was noted in the blacksmith's workshop nearby, that specialized in the production of fighting cock spurs. The anvil placed perpendicularly, is about a meter from the hearth with the water trough to the right side of the blacksmith. With the hearth to the left of the blacksmith and the anvil in front of him, the blacksmith's assistant is on the other side of the anvil. In this arrangement, the blacksmith's assistant is opposite the bellows which he operates and therefore it means that he has to walk a few steps before he can reach the bellows.

3.3.2 Secondary Structures and Equipment

The activities of moulding metal, fitting handle and case, grinding and polishing the blade, and tempering among others, are considered as secondary processes for these are done after the tool has been formed. Residue from these secondary processes are distinguishable from the primary process of tool manufacturing.

1. The Grinding and Polishing Machine. The secondary processes of grinding and polishing give the tool a sharp edge and clean even surface. There are two ways in which the process is done, by electricity and by hand.

The grinding/polishing method which is run by electricity is the more modern and the most prevalent method (Figures 23, 24, 25). It is composed of two rotating carborundum-coated grindstones powered by electricity. Circular-shaped grinders with holes in the middle are attached to rotating metal holders. These are permanently secured to a wooden or metal frame near a small post where an electrical outlet is attached.

The traditional way of grinding and polishing tools is by hand. In this method the tool is anchored flat on a table with a home-made vise grip. The surface is polished by a scraping motion using a metal file on the surface of the tool. The scraping is continued until a smooth surface is obtained (Figure 26).

Given the nature of the process where metal is given a smooth and even finish, the residue is made-up of fine metal particles, carborundum powder, and paste.

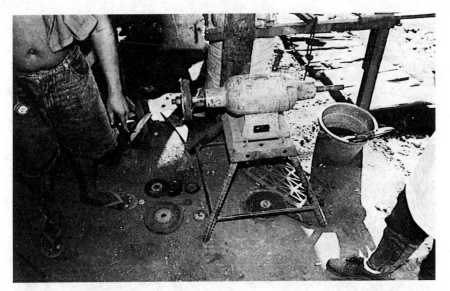

Figure 23. Circular-shaped grinders with holes in the middle attached to rotating metal holders

Figure 24. A young man grinding the shank of a bolo

Figure 25. *Another man on the other end of the electric grinder working on the back of a bolo*

Figure 26. *The traditional way of grinding where the tool is anchored flat on a table and scrape to form with the use of metal file*

The paste is used to glue the abrasive powder to the grinding/polishing wheel of the machine. The residues are deposited directly under the wheel and around it for approximately 40 centimeters from the center of the deposit. The deposit can be discerned by a hardened surface with grayish color. Over a period of time due to exposure to water and/or moisture, color turns to rusty gray. This was particularly observed in the shop of Mr. Romulo Abarquez where his abandoned grinding/polishing area was exposed in cross-section by a canal dug at the edge of the workshop where the equipment was placed.

The residue of the traditional method will have the same composition as the electric run, although other than fine metal particles, one can also find very thin metal chips and wood dust. Since unlike the former where the surface is slowly refined by friction with the abrasive, in the traditional method uneven surface is evened out by scraping the surface thinly producing metal hips. After scraping the surface it is followed by rubbing the tool surface with abrasive wheel. Since this is done on the same table where wood is also worked, the composition of residue will also indicate the presence of wood.

2. The Mold Molding is the process of forming metal into a desired shape by a prepared mold. It is done beside the furnace since aluminum and bronze need a constant temperature to be maintained for these metals to remain in a liquid state. The mold itself is made of heavy aluminum. It is composed of two opposite parts of the desired shape, with a hollow in the middle into which molten metal is poured. A clamp holds the two parts together after molten metal is poured in to allow the two opposite parts to fuse and harden.

These molds are used for some parts of the hunting knife and some parts of the handle of the samurai sword. For this purpose the mold comes in two sizes. A large mold is needed for the base of the knife and the samurai sword where the blade meets the handle. A smaller mold is used for the posterior end of the handle. An improvised scoop made of a tin can, held by tongs, is used to pour molten metal to the mold. After use the tin cans are discarded.

3. The Furnace. Of the workshops studied, melting of metal is done in Silva Workshop. The furnace is located in the eastern section of the

workshop near the concrete wall and a little bit away from constant traffic of people going into the southern side of the workshop where bellows are placed. The furnace is a chamber that is dug into the workshop floor. The walls of the furnace are made of a clay mixture similar to the kind used for the hearth wall. In cross-section, the shape is conical with a flat bottom and carinate (angled, reeled or ridged) wall. The carinate side is 15 centimeters from top (Figure 27). The bottom of the furnace serves as a catchment for ashes and a depository of charcoal for fuel. The carinated portion on top is where metal strips are laid and it functions as a platform for the crucible. It is also on this part that the *tuyere* from the electric blower heat to provide streams of air into the charcoal.

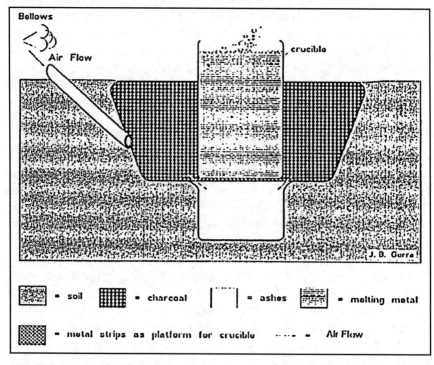

Figure27. Illustration of Furnace

Once the platform is in place, the crucible is set on top and metal (bronze and aluminum) to be melted is placed inside. Charcoal is shoveled around the container. Fire is started and maintained through the continuous blasts of air from the electric blower.

Every now and then, burnt charcoal is stoked in order to push ashes to the bottom of the furnace before new charcoal is put in. During the melting process, the crucible is covered with plain galvanized iron with a handle to keep the ashes from the metal. The melting metal is stirred occasionally and more bronze or aluminum added if necessary. Impurities in the melted metal, and ashes from the charcoal which are inadvertently deposited into the crucible while the charcoal is added to the hearth, are skimmed off with the aid of a tin can. The ashes, which are very powdery and grayish-green in color, are dumped beside the mouth of the furnace. Since the metal used is recycled from scrap materials there is no slag associated with this activity. In fact metal drippings from the mold are melted again.

4. Equipment for Handle and Case Making. Since this activity is considered a secondary function, its activity area is located at the periphery of the workshop. The workplace includes the following inventory of movable structures: a low wooden bench, a table where the vise grip is mounted, a slab of wood used as a chopping block, metal saw, *pesao*, *hudhud*, and wood drill (Figures 28 + 29).

The low wooden bench has a small rectangular wood block nailed toward one end, at the spot where the base (legs) of the bench is attached. This functions as a "stopper" (the blacksmith's term) to prevent sliding of the tool as it is shaped by the worker.

The *pesao* and *hudhud* are used here to trim and give final shape to the handle or case. The chopping wooden block is needed to stabilize the raw material, for example, guava wood, which is shaped into either handle or case especially during the initial trimming of the wood to the approximate shape with the use of a bolo. The vise grip is used in several ways: a) To hold lead pipe firmly as it is cut into rings (Figure 30); b) to hold the wood handle firmly as a hole is drilled into it to accommodate the tang; c) to hold the tool in place when a decoration is carved into the metal component.

Within the immediate area where the above-mentioned structures are, one can find plenty of wood shavings and very fine sawdust from the worked wood.

Figure 28. Wooden materials are cut to desired length

Figure 29. The wood is carved to accommodate bolo blade

Figure 30. Bolo handles as shown in picture. Vise-grip anchors the wood in place for boring a hole to hold the tang

5. The Water Trough. The water trough is also used for a secondary process, tempering. Tempering is the process of reducing the degree of hardness and brittleness and so increase toughness by immersion of hot metal in water. It removes the brittleness from a hardened piece and gives it a more fine-grained structure.

3.4 Maintenance of Equipment

Maintenance is a key to the smooth functioning of the equipment in the workshop. Before the start of every working day, all the equipment is checked by the blacksmith or his assistant. The hearth and furnace need the most maintenance.

Repair of the Hearth. (Figure 31)
The accumulation of *tambacong* not only obstructs air blasts from the bellows but also narrows the space between the walls of the hearth thus

necessitating its removal every workday particularly when production is high. *Tambacong* blockage of the *tuyere* lessens the heat of the hearth which is indicated by reddish fire. Once this is observed by the blacksmith or his assistant, the hole is pried open with a metal fire hook to remove the obstruction. This specifically happens more often when the production rate is high.

The removal of *tambacong* and subsequent repair of the hearth wall is simple and straightforward. First, the *tambacong* adhering to the interior walls of the hearth is broken off using the flat end of the crow bar. It is then scooped out of the hearth with the use of the small shovel used in scooping charcoal during smithing.

The *tambacong* is deposited under the hearth stand or thrown into a city government garbage receptacle which is collected later in the day by a garbage disposal truck and transported to the city dumping site. The *tuyere* hole is also pried into with a stick to remove *tambacong* that might have stuck to the interior of the *tuyere* itself. To ensure that all the *tambacong* is removed, air is pumped into the hearth by the bellows.

Figure 31. Blacksmith demonstrates how to repair the hearth

When there is no obstruction, strong air blows into the hearth, stirring the ashes. A *tapak* or *hulip* is prepared from a mixture of fine clay loam and water to cover the part from where the *tambacong* was removed, or to repair cracks (Figure 32).

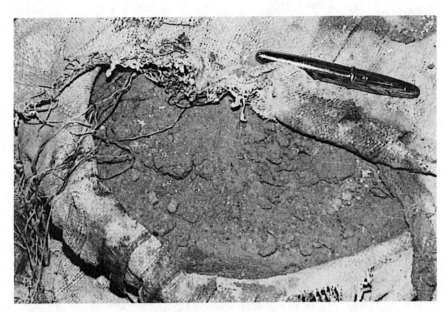

Figure 32. A sack of clay used by the blacksmith to repair or make a new hearth

This mixture is made on top of a nylon sack or a piece of plywood or galvanized iron sheet, and kneaded. The kneading is done with one hand only (for it requires less effort) to mix clay and water; small stone and limestone pieces are removed in the process. The clay is smoothed over the part where the *tambacong* was removed to replace damaged surfaces of the hearth. It is then left to dry for one hour. Sometimes some extra wet clay is left, and this is saved for the next day. During normal production the *tambacong* is removed only in the morning between 5:00 and 6:00 a.m. It has to be done at this time for it takes an hour for the clay to dry. While the clay is drying the blacksmith or his assistant can bathe, eat breakfast or prepare the necessary jobs and materials for another day at the workshop. Slow drying of clay is important for durable bonding of particles. It will also then be less susceptible to cracking. In instances where a newly retouched hearth is needed immediately, the blacksmith heats a small fire to hasten the drying.

In preparation of *hulip* or *tapak*, a variation was practiced by one of the assistants. He pounded some fired clay that was first separated from the *tambacong* and included it in the *tapak* to function as a temper. He stressed that adding fired clay strengthens the mixture, making it less likely to crack. His father, who was also a blacksmith in Carcar, taught this to him.

Repair of the Furnace.

The furnace is in need of repair when cracks are seen on the walls and the *tambacong* is so thick as to cover the hole of the blower. All the *tambacong* is removed using the sharpened tip of a flat iron bar. The removed *tambacong* is gathered to the side and transported later to a trash box. Soil similar to that which is used in the repair of the hearth is used. The soil is a clay loam with very fine sandy particles using the bottom of a softdrink bottle. Large limestones and pebbles are removed in the process of pounding. Once the soil is refined, it is mixed with water to kneading consistency (not too watery nor dry but enough for soil to hold together). This is then applied to the wall of the furnace starting from the bottom and working toward the rim. As the soil is smoothed some water is also applied every now and then and leveled with the hand to achieve a smooth wall of clay. The soil is placed up to the rim of the furnace. The newly repaired furnace is left to dry naturally for an hour after which it can be used right away. The furnace is repaired on an average of once a month.

4. Ethnoarcheology as a Background for Interpretation models

4.1 The Blacksmith: Sociology and Training

In Visayan language as well as in the Tagalog speaking region of Luzon, a blacksmith is called "panday". It is also the same term used for the carpenter in the Cebuano. In the Cebuano context when one says *"mamanday ko/'ta or pandayon nato/naku"* this means *"I will build/shape or let us will build/shape (present) or we will build/shape or I will build/shape (future)"* (Figure 33).

Figure 33. Blacksmith demonstrate the first stage of smithing a bolo

The blacksmith whether viewing it from the shadows of prehistory or of today's modern society, holds a very curious place. At times he is held with a high regard and sometimes the opposite for obvious reasons. He is considered the key person in the blacksmithing workshop for without him work will not be done. He is the person who knows and decides how each tool is manufactured. He is often consulted by the customers, especially by those who bring in designs, for they want to know whether their designs can be executed, the best material that can be used, and the length of time needed to finish.[31] The Cebuano blacksmiths are therefore involved from its inception up to the time it is tempered and ready for attachment of handles.

The year round demand for finished products has made blacksmiths always busy. Entrepreneurs, blacksmith-entrepreneurs and blacksmith-turn-interpreneurs who have capital have a great advantage because they can purchase raw materials ahead of time and in bulk. Buying in bulk they get discounts, consequently making the prices of produce a bit lower. Production tends to be more efficient because the raw material is at hand and because they are able to mass-produce the tools that are most in demand.

In the workshops that were covered by this research, the blacksmiths have an average of 10 years work experience behind them. The average age that these blacksmiths started training was 17 years old. All of them were blacksmith's assistants first before becoming blacksmiths in their own right.

All blacksmiths covered in the study came from communities that have blacksmith workshops. They believed that the environment influenced their decisions to become blacksmiths. They think highly of their work as a dignified way of earning income for their respective families.

The Blacksmith's Assistant (Figure 34)
The blacksmith's assistant is a partner to the blacksmith who assists the latter in working the metal into the desired shape. According to the "oldtimers" – those blacksmiths who are over 60 years – previously the average age that blacksmith's assistants started training was 15 years of age. This is just about the age that a sledge hammer can be lifted and handled well by the trainee. Since he is a partner to the blacksmith and

---

31

later will claim to be a blacksmith, he is under the direction of the former. Today, you cannot see 15 year olds as blacksmith assistants as they are doing cleaner more attractive work such as woodcraft and shell craft or going to school. This change in values is also the impact of formal education and the common desire of the young men to have more physically lighter, well-paid blue or white collar jobs. Most of the young men in the study area consider being a blacksmith as the least in the hierarchy of jobs that they desire to enter into. It should be noted that craftsman's work is the least paid in the Philippines.

Figure 34. The blacksmith assistant or suplio is a crucial partner to the blacksmith

Teamwork is essential between the blacksmith and his assistant for communication is not by spoken language but by visual signals. The blacksmith's assistant has to watch where the blacksmith's hammer hits the metal. This is the same spot where the assistant must strike. Once the blacksmith stops hitting hard on the metal, the sign has been made that shaping is done (Figure 35).

The blacksmith checks the tool and does the final fine hammering. While the blacksmith's assistant does little hammering his responsibility is to operate the piston lever to pump air into the bellows to maintain the fire and the required heat for the metals. If more iron has to be heated, the blacksmith's assistant collects these from the space beside the hearth and puts the metal into the fire. The tools that have gone through the primary processes are placed at the bottom of the anvil ready for collection and passing to the secondary tool processors like the tool grinders/finishers and case/handle makers.

Figure 35. Photo illustrate the cutting of molye to three equal strips of metal to be formed and shaped to three tools

4.2 The Raw Material

The blacksmiths of the study area use the *molye* (Figure 36) which is a flat bar of vehicles to manufacture their tools. They have never smelted the iron themselves but make use of the scrap metals.

Figure 36. The raw material of Cebuano blacksmith, the molye or flat bar with different bolo styles

4.3 The Fabrication of Tools

Ethnoarcheological research in a blacksmithing workshop is done to have an understanding of the dynamics of the creation of blacksmithing archaeological sites, to observe how residues are deposited on the ground, making marks significant to the archaeological record. This will help to predict patterns of archeological residues.

This part will focus on explicating the patterning of the archeological formation process by describing tool production from the cutting of raw material to the emergence of the product ready for the market. To be outlined are the different steps in producing the finished product, including the forging of tools, buffing or polishing of tools, handle and case attachment, tempering, and finally packaging of the product for the market.

To orient the reader to the description of tools, a drawing of a bladed tool is included labeled with the names of the parts for easier understanding of the text (Figure 37). This description of the process of tool production will be classified according to the process categories outlined earlier in the primary and secondary processes. Forging of blades and buffing/polishing of blades belong to the primary processes while in the secondary processes belong the handle and case attachment, and the tempering of the tools.

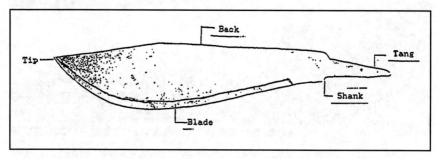

Figure 37. Parts of the bolo as identified by the blacksmiths of Cebu.

The different steps of producing bladed tools, such as the bolo, weeder or *guna*, kitchen knives, some hand tools like the pick mattock, and the *bara de cabra* (metal bar with a hold at one end) and other types including the samurai sword, sold as a novelty item, were all directly observed by the researcher in Basak.

The blacksmiths in Cebu are major recyclers of scrap metals. The raw material predominantly used by them is the flat spring bar, from trucks and cars locally known as *molye* (Figure 36). It has a length of 56 centimeters, a width of five centimeters and a thickness of 0.7 centimeters. It is preferred for it has a high concentration of iron that makes it very workable and durable, too, aside from the fact that the spring bars can be easily obtained from scrap metal dealers.

4.3.1 Primary Process in the Forging of Blades

The Cebu Bolo.

The bolo or machete is a versatile tool that the people of the Philippines have produced and valued for its wide range of application from the kitchen to the farm and as a weapon. Four bolo types are customarily made, *mistiso*, *tamway*, *boo*, and *pinoti*. These are typical Cebuano bolo styles.

To manufacture a bolo, the first step is to heat the entire spring bar to make it more malleable and easier to cut. Once heated, characterized by a reddish-orange glow, the blacksmith takes it away from the fire to the anvil. Here on the anvil the shape of the bolo is cut from the metal with the use of a cold chisel.

For the *mistiso* type bolo, cutting is diagonal to allocate a larger amount of material for the blade (Figure 38). For the other types, the cutting is vertical for the blades must be of regular width. The blades are divided lengthwise, using a cold chisel, into the number of bolos possible from the one piece of raw material. From the blacksmith's experience, the *mistiso* (Figure 39) and *boo* (Figure 40) type consume more, for from one scrap metal only two can be made, while *tamway* style allows three finished pieces. Once the cutting into individual tools is done, the metal is collected and bunched together in such a way that all handle parts are together, for it is the tang and shank portion that are heated in the hearth and shaped first.

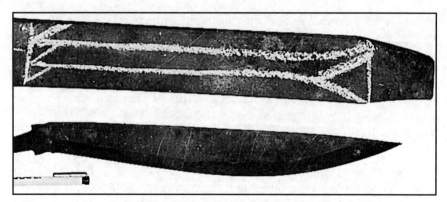

Figure 38. A piece of flatbar with lines drawn to show the number of bolos that a piece of flatbar can produce

Figure 39. The tamway bolo type and its raw material cut

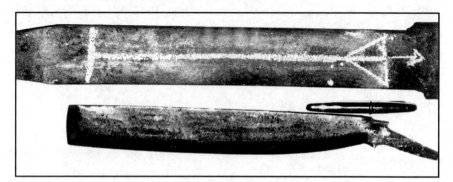

Figure 40. The boo, a bolo type specialized for splitting bamboo poles

Heat is continuously supplied to the hearth by pumping the bellows. The metal is heated until a glowing reddish-orange color is reached, then the blacksmith's assistant stops pumping air and moves to the anvil to pick up the sledge hammer. The blacksmith at the same time retrieves the heated metal using the tongs and together with the blacksmith assistant he shapes the tang and the shank. The angular portion of the shank is formed by putting the metal against the edge of the anvil and hitting it with a blacksmith's hammer to form the slight waist of the bolo. After the tang is shaped the metal is returned to the fire; this time the opposite portion is heated and this time it is the back and blade portions that are shaped. Again, once the metal has a glowing reddish-orange color the blacksmith takes each blade from the fire to the anvil and works to shape the blade. When an expansion of the blade width is desired, the round head of the sledge hammer is wielded by the blacksmith's assistant to pound the metal. The blows go straight onto the metal with the motion of pulling sidewise toward the blade portion.

To increase the length of metal, the blacksmith's assistant uses the oval shaped side of his sledge hammer. The motion of the blows is straight down onto the metal with the motion of pulling towards him (the assistant). The shaping of the tool is done by the blacksmith using a smaller hammer. Once the desired tool shape is achieved, the metal is returned to the fire for final heating and at this point of the process only the cutting edge is finally shaped and outlined. There are instances that trimming metal is also done to get rid of tiny excess metal pieces and for this purpose a cold chisel is used.

It has been observed that in this process of annealing the tools, metal exfoliates are deposited on the ground around the anvil. The exfoliation of metal only happens at this stage of tool production and therefore marks this phase of blacksmithing activity clearly.

The Bolo for Weeding. (Figure 41)
The *guna*, to mean weed, as the name implies-is use to remove weeds is a square-tipped tool. Its tip is used with a scraping motion into surface soil to uproot the weeds. Blacksmiths and farmers differentiate certain *guna* tips for different types of soil or surface. The bolo on the other hand, can be used to scrape weeds off at the surface thus preventing soil disturbance

and erosion. Both tools are heavily utilized by the agricultural sector as farming implements.

The same type of material is used for the guna, a pre-cut metal to the length of 27.3 centimeters x 3 centimeters, using a cold chisel. One end is cut diagonally to serve as the tang. Waste metal of approximately one centimeter wide pieces is deposited at the bottom of the anvil.

Figure 41. The guna, tool type and the cutting outline on the flatbar

The cut metal is bunched together and the diagonal end is placed to the fire. Air is pumped into the hearth by the blacksmith assistant once the metal is heated. The first to be hammered is the lower half of the tang and a start is made to shape the pointed tip of the tang. The shank is shaped next and then the entire tang. Once the tang is made, the other half of the metal is returned to the hearth and heated. The blade is shaped first, then the back of the bolo is aligned. In some instances the tip of the weeder is trimmed to achieve a square tip. The trimmings are tiny, thin strips of metal. Once the blades are done, the back of the weeder is checked to make sure that it is straight and not twisted. When a little twisting is observed, the tool is hammered until aligned.

The Bolo with Curved Tip

The curve-tipped bolo is called *lagaraw* or *lampas* (Figure 42) in Cebuano. Like the *weeder*, this tool is predominantly used in agricultural activity, especially in sugarcane plantations. It is useful in the trimming of sugar cane leaves during harvest. The curved tip is especially handy for using as a hook to gather together the leaves and harvested sugar cane stems.

The production of this tool follows the steps described above except for the curving. For this, while the blade is being shaped, it is gradually elongated by using the oval-shaped side of the sledge hammer. The assistant directs the blow toward him with a pulling motion. As the tip is elongated it is also curved by alternately hammering and pushing the back of the tool against the edge of the anvil to get the curve desired. This curving of the tool is done by the blacksmith assistant.

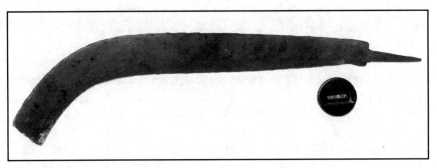

Figure 42. The lampas, a farming tool used to cut sugarcane or high-growing weeds like cogon

The Hunting Knife.

The production of the hunting knife deviates a little from the other blade tools for after the blade is done, the molding of metal components follows, then it is ground. The flat spring is cut into pieces with a width of 2.5–2.8 millimeters and a length of 35.6 centimeters. The pieces are heated one after another, for each, the ends are cut diagonally. The blade is indented with the hammer and left to cool. Once cooled, the indentations are hammered on the reverse side to separate the metal projections from each other and produce long and thin metal strips with diagonal ends. A bunch of blades are collected by the blacksmith and placed in the hearth and covered with charcoal. Fire is hastened by the pumping of the bellows by the blacksmith's assistant. Once a glowing red (more than redorange) color is seen in the metal, the blades are retrieved one by one from the fire. First to be worked up is the blade edge, which is rounded and smoothed. The top-edge (back) angle is also shaped. As the blacksmith and blacksmith's assistant are working on the tool, the tool is bent a little downwards so that the assistant does not get burnt with the glowing metal that exfoliates from the worked tool. The hammering is done horizontally flat against the anvil to achieve a well aligned tool with an even surface.

The Samurai Sword.
The samurai sword is not a indigenous tool to the Philippines. It is produced in Silva's Hunting Knife Shop as a souvenir item. Production began in an era when during the movies about Japanese warriors become popular (1980s). Since then, the demand has continued. Even it is a souvenir item, the tool can also be used as a weapon.

The samurai sword comes in three sizes, large, medium and small. To produce a samurai, the first step is to cut the raw material into the desired length. The length for large is 30 centimeters, medium 20 centimeters, and small 15 centimeters. The width of the raw material is cut into four equal parts. One end of the raw material is cut diagonally, producing a triangular metal waist and a diagonal tip. The other end, opposite the cut of the triangular tip, is heated first and then worked to a square liked shape. The unworked portion is returned to the fire and worked in the same way as the posterior. The tang of the samurai is attached later through welding.

The Pick-mattock
The pick-mattock is used in breaking the soil surface for gardening. To produce the tool, the flat spring metal is cut crosswise to the length of 14 centimeters. At one end of this rectangular metal piece, a triangular shape is cut out starting from the side edge and meeting halfway in the middle of the raw material, forming a triangle. This small triangular shaped metal piece is deposited at the bottom of the anvil as waste. The blade is then heated and the tapered half is shaped first to a thin cutting edge. After being returned to fire, the other, wide half is flattened and the edge is shaped. While shaping the cutting edge, the blacksmith elevates the other end, the wide end of tool, against the anvil to achieve a slightly curved surface.

4.3.2 Secondary Process in the Completion of Metal Tools

Grinding and Polishing.
After the tools are forged, the surface has to be rid of nicks and hammer dents. This is where the grinding/polishing machine is of use. First, the uneven surface of the finished tool is trimmed to a smooth and even surface. Second, the blade boundary is shaped and the blade edge is trimmed to a thin cutting edge.

The grinding/polishing machine is composed of two rotating carborundum-covered whetstones attached to each other by rotating metal rods anchored in a wooden structure near a post where the electric outlet is located. This type is an improvisation of the commercially manufactured one which comes with a stand and is also run by electricity (please see Figures 24 & 25). The grinding/polishing machines have adjustable plates to allow the person operating them to change the grade (from large to fine) to suit to the requirement of the tool being polished.

In the past, polishing tools by grinding was usually the first job that any aspiring blacksmith did. Today, this may not be the case for workshop workers tend to specialize due to the high production requirement,

Prior to grinding/polishing, the tool is coated with cooking oil to reduce or minimize friction that can lead to overheating of metal and cause cracks. First to be worked is the blade edge which is thinned out and shaped evenly starting from the blade line to the blade edge. This is followed by the grinding of the back of the bolo to a smooth and even surface. Then the rest of the surface of the tool is also polished. Every once in a while the tools are dipped in water to cool them and therefore prevent the metal from cracking due to brittleness as a consequence of overheating.

Before the advent of electricity powered grinding/polishing machines, the blacksmiths polished the tools by hand. The instruments used were the vise grip, pieces of wood, draw knife, flat scraper and file.

To be polished, a tool is anchored to a vise grip (please Figure 26) and reinforced with a piece of wood to make it unmovable. A draw knife is used to scrape the surface by shaving and paring rough slices of metal.

This is followed by a flat scraper that removes the remaining flaws. The cutting edge of the blade is thinned out using a file.

Handle Attachment.
The attachment of handle and case can be optional, for sometimes customers just buy *suwelto*. *Suwelto* (Figure 43) refers to the tool without handle/case attachment. This is sometimes preferred because it is cheaper and the customers make the handle themselves.

The handles used for large bladed tools such as the bolo are pre-cut to a length of 10 centimeters, just after the wood is purchased by the owner of the workshop. The wood is from the guava tree (Psidium guajava L.). This has been the traditional material, valued for its toughness due to its interlocking and swirling wood grain. The handle is first trimmed to come up with a rectangularly shaped wood that is wider at the posterior end (Figure 44). A bolo is used to trim the wood. This is followed by making of an oval-shaped mark for a metal ring at the top of the wood, using a small hammer. Once the mark is made, the wood outside the mark is chipped using the bolo. Once the approximate shape is achieved, the metal ring is then fitted into the wood using a hammer. Any excess wood that has been shaved in preparation for fitting of metal is trimmed using a metal saw applied in a light sawing manner. Holes are drilled in the middle of the metal ring about two centimeters deep (Figure 45). The tang of the bolo is heated. The heated tang is inserted into the handle and pounded against the anvil or any hard surface until it sinks up to the shank or waist against the fitted metal ring. The metal ring or *piket* (Figure 46) serves as a guard to prevent the wood from cracking, for this would loosen the tool from handle. Then the handle shape is trimmed further to make smooth the surface, first using the *pesao* to carve the angle of the handle and then the *hudhud* to complete the fine smoothing of the wood. This process of polishing the handle, using the *pesao* and *hudhud*, is done at a low workbench with a wood stopper at the end to hold the tool in position.

Figure 43. A bolo type produced by the blacksmiths in Carcar

Figure 44. A handle maker chopping a guava wood handle to shape

Figure 45. The vise-grip holds the handle in place for boring

Figure 46. The handle-maker pounded the metal ring to hold the shank in place

The hunting knife handle is a combination of lawanit and molded aluminum metal. Lawanit is produced from a mixture of sawdust and glue pressed firmly to produce a board. The metal components of the hunting knife handle are found at the base of the blade and the posterior tip of handle. These pieces serve to anchor and bond the pieces of lawanit board fitted tightly together (Figure 47). Work on the handle starts with the fitting of the aluminum component by molding (see description of molding).

Figure 47. Another version of handle using cut lawanit pieces

Once the hunting knife aluminum handle component has cooled down, it is passed to the grinders who trim the excess from the tang that sticks out from the posterior metal component. The rough and extra edges of aluminum are trimmed using a metal saw. The aluminum components are removed from the knife by clipping each knife into the vise-grip, blade toward the ground. The components are hit with a small hammer to loosen then from handle. Once the components are separated, the hunting knife is removed from the vise grip and is used to prop up the ends of the aluminum components one after the other for filing with the use of a flat metal file. When more trimming is necessary this is accomplished by using an iron saw, then filing again. When this is completed the handle components are set aside.

The handle finisher works on straightening the tang of the knife using a small anvil. The knife is secured again to the vise grip, with blade tip pointing down and the handle tip pointing upwards. The handle tip is sharpened to a point for easier insertion of the *lawanit* pieces cut into 1 x 1 inch squares. These pieces are inserted into the handle one by one. A small piece of metal pipe is used to guide the *lawanit* pieces. It is placed on top of each small lawanit piece and hit with small anvil, pushing the *lawanit* through the tang. Each piece is secured firmly to the tang, one on top of the other. As every piece is firmly placed, excess pieces of *lawanit* that protrude around the tang are trimmed off using a metal saw. Trimming is done before the next new piece is inserted. *Lawanit* pieces are inserted until a one-inch space is left from the posterior tip. This will accommodate the aluminum component. Once this component is placed it is pounded to compress the *lawanit* pieces tightly. Sometimes a part of the tip sticks out even after the component is already attached; it will later be trimmed in the grinder.

Seen scattered under and around the working table to a circumference of 60 centimeters are fine, powdery wood shavings and small pieces of *lawanit* trimming. There are discarded large pieces of *lawanit* that crack in the process and have to be discarded. Tiny pieces and powdery shavings of aluminum are also seen. The larger pieces of aluminum from the trimmings are collected and melted again for use in handle components.

The handle of the samurai sword is also a metal and wood combination. The metal is attached to the handle at the shank or waist section of the knife and at the posterior end. The attachment is done in the same manner as in the hunting knives. The molds are larger than for the hunting knife. The wood component of the handle is a softwood cut to cover two metal sides and glued in place. The metal used in this combination is bronze.

The molds used are made of heavy iron material and come with clamps to hold the upper and lower parts together. Prior to molding, the depressed interior of a crucible is brushed with oil to prevent the metal from sticking to the interior. After this, the base of the hunting knife is fitted to the crucible and the other half is placed on top; the two are fastened together with a clamp. Using a scoop, improvised from a tin can, and a long nose tongs, the worker dips the handle into the mold and pours in the molten aluminum. Since aluminum hardens immediately after pouring, the knife is immediately removed and another one is placed in the molder. The molding process is done systematically, the base of the handle is done first, and the posterior end is done last. Prior to molding at the posterior end, the knife is dipped quickly into a bucket of water to cool it. This is also done to the crucible when it approaches the melting stage itself.

Tempering
To temper the blade, the tool is placed on top of the curvilinear hump of the hearth wall (Figure 48). It is heated on a bluish fire for a few minutes. The tool is removed from the hearth by the blacksmith with a tong grasped at the tang. It is brought to the water trough where the blade edge is dipped into the water quickly. A tempered blade is indicated by a yellowish color on the blade line. Although fresh water is the most common and inexpensive source for quenching, sometimes the black-smith use powdered cyanide for the purpose. Basically it follows the procedure mentioned above but while the tool is heated the blacksmith prepare a small lump of cyanide in one sheet of newspaper. The heated tool is then carried to where the cyanide is and the blade edge is pressed slightly through the lump of cyanide. The contact of the heated metal and the cyanide give a very acrid, pungent odor. The tool is cooled by slowly pouring water starting from the blade until the entire tool is wet.

Although this way of tempering result to similar color as in the water quenched, the blacksmith believed that the latter give more sturdy metal than the former without specifically giving the reason to this observation. The use of cyanide however is dangerous because of the fumes, blacksmiths realize this and rarely use this method of tempering blades. During the entire fieldwork it was only used twice by Mulo Abarquez to on a *pinoti*.

Figure 48. Blacksmith applying water on the blade to temper the tool

Packaging (Figure 49)

Once all the handle has been attached, the product is wiped with a clean cotton cloth. The handle and case (optional) is coated with one stroke of varnish. The blade is wiped with oil. This is now ready for display. For products that are destined for shipment, these are wrapped in newspaper and placed in containers either cartoon boxes or large native transport baskets locally called *kaing*.

Figure 49. Assorted bolos with carborundum stone.

4.4 The Products: Form and Quality (Figure 50)

The bulk of the products that are produced by the blacksmiths in Basak and Carcar are utility tools for farming and well as the household. For example knives that are for chopping and slicing, bolos that comes into three different lengths to adapt to its use. The shorter ones with an average length of 35 centimeters are use for chopping wood, those with the mean length of 50 centimeters are use to chop leaves or small twigs. The third type of bolo has a special name *pinoti* (Figure 51) whose function is more of a weapon. These bolos are about a meter long and has a bald width at its widest point of about 6 centimeters. There is also a special kind of bolo with a blunt square tip called *amol* (Figure 52) that is used for splitting bamboo for make floors and walls. The *Guna* – a blunt bolo about 25 centimeters long or less with a blunt, wide tip for weeding. They also manufacture specific tools like the *sanggot* to cut budding coconut palm to extract palm wine. A variation of the sanggot use to slice the tender part of the banana trunk to feed the pigs (Figure 53). They also manufacture the acha-axe, a term used may have its origins in the Spanish occupation.

Figure 50. A typical blacksmith store with its array of products

Figure 51. A profile of pinote, a tradition Visayan weapon

Figure 52. A utilitarian bolo type used to split bamboo

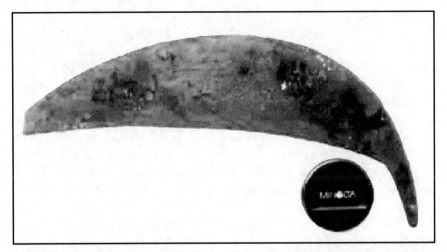

Figure 53. A utilitarian tool used to make thin slices of banana trunk or soft coconut bud

4.5 Need and Distribution of the Fabricated Tools

The year round demand for finished products has made blacksmiths always busy, more for those who have capital, for they can purchase raw materials ahead of time and in bulk. This is particularly the case for the owners of Silva's Hunting Knife Shop, Mulo Abarquez Garden Tools Supply and Carcar Workshop. As owners/managers of these workshops know the basic principles of the technology, but hire and train other blacksmiths to work for them. This way they are able to mass-produce different tools that have the most demand; they do not depend on walk-in customers. Therefore they are able to do made-to-order jobs from middlemen or business men from other places, thus expanding the market for their products.

The manager acts as the over-all coordinator of the workshop. He takes the orders of customers, sets the prices for finished materials, and oversees the raw materials needed for production. In large workshops, more often the manager is the person who put up the business. He may have some knowledge of the technology itself, but as manager may not how to produce the tools himself. Even so, he does jobs such as welding handles, grinding the finished products, and other jobs that are related to blacksmithing.

In a big workshop like Silva Shop, the manager is assisted by an overseer who helps in the supervision of production, the crew and also tends the store where the finished products are displayed for walk-in customers. In small workshops on the other hand more often the manager is also the blacksmith.

The reputation of the fine craftsmanship of the Cebuano blacksmiths is widely known in the Visayas and even in Mindanao particularly the Northern part-most migrants come from the Visayan area. As rule, their products are widely distributed and desired especially in areas where agriculture is the predominant way of life. The presence of these smithed products must be deeply ingrained in the culture of the Visayan or even in the Filipino culture as a whole. If one does not have a bolo in the household, then one must be so poor to afford it. This indigenous value orientation of this utility tool reflect how these tools were necessary for the survival of a people before the introduction of modern technology. So it is common practice in Cebu that if anyone wants to have practical utility tools around the house one goes to Basak, Carcar, Consolacion or Lilo-an all in Cebu.

5. Analysis of Slag

In the Philippine archaeological sites the prevalence of the recovery of slags is a fact that cannot be ignored. They are quoted in almost all reports and appears in the artifact inventory record of the National Museum of the Philippines. To mention a few examples were those collected from the Languile site,Taal Batangas; Manggahan sites in Baag, San Marcelino,Zambales; Torralba-Sanchez sites, Butuan City; Panhutungan site, Placer, Surigao del Norte, recently excavated by Dr. Eusebio Dizon[32]; Burauen, Leyte of A. Barbosa[33]; Santa Ana site in Manila of R. Fox and A. Legaspi[34]; Tanjay, Negros Oriental sites of L. Junker[35]; Pila, Laguna[36] Puerto Galera sites of R. Tenazas[37] and sites of Cebu Archaeological Project by M Nishimura[38], to quote a few from a much more comprehensive list.

---

32   Dr. Eusebio Dizon, archaeologist, National Museum of the Philippines, (pers. comm.). Dr. Dizon is the current authority on Philippine archaeometallurgy and the metal age.

33   Artemio Barbosa, "Archaeological Exploration and Excavation in Burauen, Leyte," Leyte-Samar Studies, Vol. 12 no. 2 (1978), pp. 27–40.

34   Dr. Robert B. Fox and Avelino Legaspi, *Excavation at Santa Ana*, National Museum of the Philippines, Manila (1977).

35   Dr. Laura L. Junker, "The Organization of Intra-Regional and Long Distance Trade in Pre-hispanic Philippine Complex Societies" (paper presented at the Society for American Archaeology meetings, April 2–9, 1989, Atlanta, Georgia).

36   Rosa P. Tenazas, *A Report on the Archaeology of the Locsin-University of San Carlos Excavations in Pila, Laguna.* (September 4, 1967 – March 19, 1968).

37   Tenazas, Rosa, "The Salvage Excavation of Southern Luzon, Philippines: A Summary," *Philippine Quarterly of Culture and Society* Vol. I No. 2 (1973), pp. 132–136.

38   Masao Nishimura, "Long Distance Trade and the Central Philippines – The Cebu Archaeological Project: Basic Concepts and First Results," *Philippine Quarterly of Culture and Society*, Vol. 16 (1988) pp. 107–157.

In view of the prevalence of these artifacts in the inventory of recovered materials, there is a need to strengthen the information on the context in which these slags are generated. The purpose of ethnoarchaeology is to examine from a contemporary materialistic point of view, the variable conditions/situations that an artifact can be produced to prevent inaccurate or sweeping conclusions. This is where semi-quantitative analysis becomes helpful. The blacksmith slag sample *tambacong* was found at the interior walls of the hearth in the immediate and opposite part of the tuyere. This residue based on field observation is only formed with the heating of hearth and furnace in a blacksmith workshop. The sample was obtained from the interior wall of a hearth. It was broken off for the researcher by the blacksmith using the flat end of a crow bar during regular maintenance of the hearth.

To look into the morphology of the blacksmith slag, the Scanning Electron Microscope was used and EDAX. EDAX is a method of employing X-ray spectrography. It is based on the principle that samples are subjected to X-ray photons which produce photoelectrons through ionization. The amount of photoelectrons produced is specific for each element. A calcium X-ray is about 3.7 kilo-electron volts (kev) equivalent to approximately a thousand electrons, while a nickel X-ray gives about two thousand electrons. Thus, elements can be identified by counting the electrons. However, the analysis is far more complicated than this text has room for[39].

Comparison of slag surface morphology
From the surface morphology alone it can be inferred that the matrice of the blacksmith slag as an ethnoarchaelogical sample has no crystalline structure. Its glass bubbles exhibit a homogenous glass matrix. This amorphic glass texture is viscous even at high magnifications of x1063 and x1286. The gas bubbles range from 2 micron to 250 microns in circumference. Also, minute crystals from 1 to 10 microns in size can be observed.

They represent early crystallization stages wherein certain elements are enriched. Thus, cooling of these samples must have occurred rapidly

---

39   John C. Russ *Principles of EDAX Analysis on the Electron Microscope* Lecture and Workshop Notes, EDAX International, Inc. 1976.

so that the atomic oxides could not be arranged into minerals with a certain crystal geometry. At the interfaces of the gas bubbles and the glass matrix, minute coatings can be detected, suggesting a selective enrichment of iron. Moreover, at the gas matrix itself, isolated minute crystals can be observed. Unlike the observed coatings, these crystals are enriched with chromium, iron, potassium, gold and aluminum as indicated by EDAX analysis.

The conspicuous features in both the archaeological and ethno-archaeological are the bubbles of gas. The more SiO_2 in a sample, the more gas bubbles since the silicious contents make it very viscous. This means that the gas content, for example CO_2 and water vapor, cannot leave the sample when it cools down to become solid rock.

The presence of CL- (Chlorine) and F- (Flourine) indicates that the pressure in the samples is so low that the halogens cannot be integrated with the minerals. When a molten material cools fast, as here, many small bubbles form, while when molten material cools slowly, bubbles will be less numerous but larger, as in magmatic/volcanic rocks.

Archeological Sample: Lapu-lapu Street Site

For the archeological sample window sets for 0–8,000 kev; spot analysis of glass surface revealed that at 0–8,000 kev silicon(Si), potassium(K),chlorine(Cl), iron (Fe), manganese(Mn), sodium(Na), calcium(Ca) and titanium(Ti) were observed, at 0–15.000 kev significant peaks of silicon(Si), palladium(Pd), alumminum(Al) and gold(Au). The presence of silicon and aluminum peaks show that molten clay/silicates minerals form the most important portion of the supposedly smelted material. Gold and palladium peaks may be due to the contamination by sputtering, although the spot analysis was done on an uncoated surface. Remarkable also is the abundance of alkaline and alkaline earth elements such as sodium, potassium, calcium and manganese. The chlorine might be attributed to seawater contamination sine the Lapu-lapu Street excavation was only ten meters away from the old coastline of Cebu.

Ethnoarcheological Sample: Basak

Window sets for magnifications of 0–20,000 kev spot analysis matrix and spot analysis gas bubble window set at 0–15,000 kev magnifications showed the following:

a) Significant peaks of silver (Ag), aluminum (Al), iron (Fe), manganese (Mg), titanium (Ti), and gold (Au) were observed at 0–20,000 kev.
b) Significant peaks of silicon (Si), iron (Fe), magnesium (Mg), manganese (Mn), silver (Ag), potassium (K), calcium (Ca), titanium (Ti), and gold (Au) were shown at 0–15,000 kev.

The first EDAX mapping above showed a peak of gold probably brought about by contamination during preparation of the sample rather than by the natural element occurring in the site. The second observation shows silicon(Si), aluminum(Al) peaks. These must reflect the clay mineral contributions to the molten ethnoarchaeological material taken from the blacksmith's hearth in Basak. Also, potassium(K), and calcium(Ca) belong to the alkaline earth group elements common in certain clay minerals or derived from the carbonate contents of clay. Such carbonate rock is common in the Carcar limestone of Cebu Island. Clay minerals belong to the phyllosilicate group. Kaolinite and montmorillonite are the most common clay minerals in Cebu, with the latter being more abundant. Kaolinite – Al_4 $\{(OH)_8$ Si_4 $O_{10}\}$ is more or less a pure aluminum hydrosilicate while Montmorillonite ($Al_{1.67}$ $Mg_{0.33}$) $\{(OH)_2$ Si_4 $O_{10}\}^{0.33}$ $Na_{0.33}$ $(H_2O)_4$ is chemically much more complex. Aside from aluminum cations, sodium (Na) and manganese (Mn) are also present. However, aluminum (Al), sodium (Na) and manganese (Mg) can be exchanged against other cations. Since aluminum (Al), sodium (Na), and manganese (Mg) have prominent peaks in our samples. Montmorillonite is most probably the source for it is the most abundant clay mineral in Cebu. This conclusion is justified by the actual ethnoarchaeological observation that blacksmiths use soil in the construction and repair of their hearths in Basak.

Montmorillonite forms small crystals which cannot be observed even with a strong light microscope. This explains why no crystals were seen in the surface morphology. Water is lost in the interlayers of the crystal at 100 to 250 degrees Celsius. The constitutional water of the crystal disappears at temperatures between 670 to 700 degrees Celsius which mark consisting mainly of montmorillonite crystals is most likely melted in the blacksmith workshops in Basak, thereby contaminating the slag-like material with droplets of the beginning of melting[40]. This means that a soil overheated iron. Such temperatures prepared for our specimen can be inferred from the glowing red color of the iron being heated[41] in Basak hearths indicating that 1,550 degrees Celsius are reached here.

The bonding patterns of aluminum(Al) and silicon(Si) strongly suggest that the origin of both slag materials was a silicate mineral which is more abundant than iron. This observation is further strengthened by the analyses conducted on the matrices show that this material is not an iron slag as a product of smelting but derive from silicon minerals because of the abundance of alkaline and alkaline earth metals. The iron is not homogenously distributed in the slag materials (glass) but concentrated at the interfaces of the glass matrices and the glass bubbles for the Basak sample. The possible source of these droplets of metal are iron tools heated in the hearths, where small particles start to melt and adhere to molten clay.

---

40   Rudolf Hohl (ed.), *Die Entwicklungsgeschichte der Erde*, 5th Edition (1981). Dausien, Hanau.

41   John L. Feirer, *op. cit*, 214.

6. Interpretation of Techniques and Summary

This is an ethnoarchaeological type of research. It is used in understanding the dynamics of the creation of blacksmithing archaeological sites especially predicting patterns of archaeological residues. This is determined by elucidating the behavior patterns in the smithing processes which are debris-generating and that make significant contributions to the archaeological record of blacksmithing sites. The focus of this study were the two blacksmith workshops in Basak, Cebu City. The workshops were mapped to show the exact location of each structure and equipment and the type of debris that it deposits on the ground. Informal interviews were also conducted of the members of the smithing workshops as to the different steps involved in tool production.

This research has substantiated that in the Cebuano blacksmithing shop, tool-making activities form residues that are archaeologically relevant. The findings of the study are summarized as follows:

1.0 To clearly elucidate the debris generating behavior of blacksmithing, the work processes of tool production were classified into two categories, primary and secondary. Both these processes have produced significant presence in the archaeological context.

1.1 The forge which comprises the hearth, anvil, water trough and bellows is where the primary activities take place. It is the site for the process of cutting and shaping of a tool. Among the parts of the forge that generate archaeological residues are the hearth and the anvil.

1.2 In the secondary work process, the smithing activities of polishing/ grinding the metal, attachment of handle/case, and the furnace, all form residues are to be archaeologically relevant. Bearing in mind that the techniques of soil analysis is so well developed that different organic substances can be identified.

2.0 The workflow of tool production starts with the forging of the tool, after which it is polished in the grinding/polishing machine, and followed by the attachment of handle and/or case for the bolo and other similar tools. A variation for hunting knives is the molding of metal components after which lawanit squares are inserted one by one. Finally the tool is tempered. Bearing in mind the workflow mentioned above, there is a marked difference in the residue variation. The variations of the work process residue in the workflow of smithing activities can be distinguished as follows:

2.1 The forging (cutting and shaping) of tools by the blacksmith is associated with thick a deposit of tiny metal wastes that are discarded during the trimming of metal prior to and after heating. They are mixed with thin metal exfoliation that occur after metal is heated and pounded to shape. Among the equipment of the forge that are directly linked to debris-generation are the hearth and anvil.

    2.1.a The hearth produces the slag-like residues locally called *tambacong*. Underneath the hearth stand one can observe that the burnt charcoal, ashes and tambacong are deposited and collected much, much later to a trash can, only when a large pile has accumulated there.

    2.1.b The bottom of the anvil will show a very heavy concentration of metal exfoliation and tiny pieces of cut metal. These are also mixed with charcoal and ashes. As a matter of fact, near this type of debris there are also thick deposits of charcoal, ashes and some slag-like material or *tambacong*.

    2.1.c The slag-like artifact tambacong, mentioned above, is the residue from the hearth and the furnace. The *tambacong* is probably a combination of molten clay and metal which due to high temperature in the hearth has fused. This is the only residue that is linked with the heat-generating equipment of blacksmithing. This is a significant finding since traditionally, artifacts that look like the tambacong are reported in Philippine archaeological reports as a product of smelting. These observations will have to be substantiated by further test.

    2.1.d The workfloor of the forge is black in color due to charcoal stain. The stain comes from the spilling of charcoal and charcoal dust on the ground in the process of pouring charcoal from the sack to the charcoal container beside the hearth. Additionally, the burnt charcoal deposited under the hearth spills onto the forging area floor.

2.2   In the space underneath the rotating carborundum wheel is deposited a fine residue composed of metal, carborundum surface, and paste. The mixture of these three substances with moisture from the air or water is sprinkled on the space to subdue dust and ashes, produce a hardened matrix on the floor. After a period of time this deposit turns a reddish brown color due to oxidation of iron. In fact, in the Abarquez workshop an abandoned grinding/polishing area was observed which makes a very visible mark in the stratigraphic profile. The surface is so compact and hard that it is difficult to penetrate it with a ballpen tip.

2.3   The space where the wooden handle/case attachment is done will have tell-tale signs of the activity by the deposition of wood dust. Since the large pieces of wood shavings are carried to a refuse container and the area swept with the use of coconut fronds, the only sign will be those fine particles – wood dust, that are a result of wood shaving. This may not be visible to the naked eye but a flotation and soil composition analysis can detect this type of residue. A variation of residues from handle attachment is from the handle attachment of the hunting knife, where fine powdery sawdust and small pieces of lawanit trimming mixed with tiny particles of aluminum shavings are laid down. These will also be interspersed with some large pieces of discarded lawanit.

3.0   The only modification that has been observed as far as the work floor of the blacksmith shop is concerned is related to the area where the blacksmith and/or his assistant stands. Where the anvil is at a slightly lower elevation than the users stands, the soil at the bottom of the anvil is scraped or dug to a depth that is comfortable for standing. The opposite is done when the anvil is higher. The modification is done by either scraping the soil or filling the standing space with soil. Smithing activities will result in modifications of the work-space floor.

4.0   Based on the observation of blacksmithing activity, only the primary activity will have a specific location within the workshop since all of its equipments are firmly anchored in the ground. Also this is the only structure where the roof is a necessity. The anchoring of the grinding/polishing machine is only done in the Silva shop. All the other secondary tools are movable and their location can be subject to the moods of the workers as far as their comfort is concerned.

Variations are observed in the arrangement of the primary equipment. In the Silva workshop, the anvil is placed perpendicularly to the hearth and bellows such that only a step is needed (if any) for the blacksmith and his assistant to move from the anvil to the hearth and back. In the Abarquez workshop, the blacksmith has to walk to the hearth from the anvil and vice versa. In Carcar, due to the availability of space, both the blacksmith and his assistant have to walk from the anvil to the hearth and bellows respectively and back to the anvil. This shows that density of a population may play a role in the arrange of a workshop as seen in Cebu.

5.0 Primary activities and secondary activities lead to the formation of specific, archaeologically distinguishable locations within the workshop, is borne out.

It was observed that in the workshops studied, the forge was located in the center and around it were different secondary tools that were portable, on the periphery or fringes of the workshop. The primary activity (metal cutting to shaping of tool in the smithing) was always done under a roof. This is necessary since the tools were non-portable and too heavy to be carried to a shelter in case it rains, unlike the secondary structures that are quite handy. Besides, the parts of the forge needed a steady support to anchor them well, since much force is applied in the process of forging a tool. This also points to the fact that the forge is the most important part of smithing since it is here the tool is cut and shaped. It is also the first equipment that has to be understood by any blacksmith to be able to start his life's work. Primary activities of blacksmithing have a more central location than secondary process in the manufacture of the tools.

Implications of the Findings for the Archaeological Record
Among the debris that are likely to enter and remain in the archaeological record, given the nature of the archaeological activity and the dynamic

processes involved in tool production, one can most likely expect the following:

1. The primary equipment will be clearly distinguished because of a heavy concentration of ash, burnt charcoal and tambacong mixed into the pile. Near this, within a maximum range of 2 meters, will also be the decayed metal exfoliation and some metal pieces, and near them will be a depression in the soil noted by the difference in the matrix.
2. In the secondary equipment the debris most likely to enter the archaeological record is the residue from grinding/polishing, and the activities related to handle/case attachment which will give the soil matrix a dark color due to decay in inorganic material like wood. And finally the furnace will clearly show up together with its associated tambacong deposits on the furnace wall.
3. The results of both the SEM and EDAX analysis suggests that the archaeological sample could have had the same origin as that of the Basak sample. That means from the blacksmith's hearth and not that of the smelter.
4. The other aims of the study: to explore production center, source and origin of iron and the production and distribution of blacksmith goods, data was gathered through secondary information from secondary literature and as well as interview with the blacksmiths on the oral history of their craft.
   4.1 Based on the written literature that the researcher has accessed, blacksmithing was practices in Cebu at Spanish contact. In turn, the Spanish Chroniclers mentioned that Cebu port was actively trading with the Chinese, iron and gold were ones of the items of trade. In fact based on these records, iron was traded by the local population with the Spanish for gold-making iron more valuable than gold. Basak is the best candidate to the origin of blacksmithing in Cebu because it near the coastal area where prehispanic Cebuanos built there settlement. This is located in San Nicolas the first known town in the Philippines, therefore making consequently the oldest town in the country and the first parish in Cebu. Information based on interviews with the blacksmiths in Cebu and oral history through the interviews with old people who are indigenous to Cebu, that the researcher met in

the process of the research often made reference to Basak, making it synonymous with blacksmithing.

Looking into the language of the Cebuano, there is no specific term for a blacksmithing, but rather it adapts a term to denote a craft which shape and build materials called *panday*. *Panday (carpenter, Zimmermann)* in the native language can refer to a group of craftsmen who build from houses to boats. Boat-building industry was part and parcel of Visayan life being located in an environment surrounded by water.

4.2 Based on the geological data available and in personal communication with Dr. P. Büchsel, a geologist, that although Cebu may have copper, gold and silver. These are found kilometer below the surface that, without the modern techniques of mining is not within reach nor direct exploitation by the native population.

4.3 The smithed products are marketed not only in Cebu itself but are bought by merchants to the other islands in the Visayas and even to the island of Mindanao. Northern Mindanao according to the local smiths is also as a strong market for their products because farming is more intensively practiced. In fact, the Cebu blacksmith mentioned a few names of blacksmith who migrated to Northern Mindano.

Conclusions

Directly observing a living society permits the observation and direct assessment of how an archaeological record is being formed. The study has shown that ethnoarchaeology allows the documentation of present day behaviors of blacksmiths through the entire smithing process to see what types of debris-generating behavior are significant in the archaeological record. This way predictions can be made about how an artifact can enter the archaeological record. It is also a way of coming up with alternative explanations to the static archaeological record that the archaeologist traditionally uncovered in the process of the study of the past. It helps in interpreting the past by posting relevant questions and possible alternative explanations.

The study also shows the importance and relevance of the inter-disciplinary approach and cooperation in studying a problem. The Institute for Geology and Paleontology the analysis of the samples.

This study has also benefited from the use of historical literature gleaned from secondary sources, as well as oral accounts to offer an idea as to the origins and practice of blacksmithing technology.

Based on the findings of the study there is an urgent need to do the following recommendations to come-up with a far more lucid idea of the arguments presented in this research:

1. That further ethnoarchaeological study be done on a larger scale in Basak simultaneous with an excavation of an abandoned blacksmith shop to test the observations that were made of in a living site, and the summary just presented. This is important since with the excavation of an abandoned site we can check the observations that have been stated in the previous chapters and further help refine the method of analysis, since one could actually see how a blacksmith workshop would look as a static archaeological context. It will test the relevance of the interpretation of the living blacksmith shop as against the non-living blacksmithing archaeological site.

2. That the semi-qualitative analysis of EDAX be used again with a larger ethnographic and archaeological samples before findings presented can be held conclusive. Since the test conducted was only one sample from an ethnographic as well as one sample from archaeological site, there is a need to test more samples so that we are able to come-up with more stronger generalizations. There is a need to make comparative tests of slag from other archaeological sites in Philippines and also from other blacksmith sites in the Philippines. There is a need also to test slag from other blacksmithing sites throughout Philippines, located in different soils, and compare these with the tests of slag from archaeological sites. The interpretation offered here must be treated in a tentative way and as an alternative explanation.

3. In studies like this where a technical evaluation of a sample is necessary, there is a need for interdisciplinary cooperation and collaboration with the physical and chemical sciences.

7. Literature

Balunia, Mary Jane
1995   "Preliminary Report on the Archeological Exploration and Test Excavations of the Astillero Site, Dancalan, Donsol, Sorsogon" National Museum of the Philippines (Typscript).

Barbosa, Artemio
1978   "Archaeological Exploration and Excavation in Burauen, Leyte." *Leyte-Samar Studies* Vol.12, No 2 (1978), 27–40.

Binford, Lewis
1989   Debating Archaeology. California: New Academic Press, Inc.

Braun, Herman-Josef
1991   Das Eisenhüttenwesen des Hünsrücks: 15. bis Ende 18. Jahrhundert. Trier Historische Forschungen; Band 17. Trier.

Chen, Kwan-tzuu
2000   Ancient Technology of Taiwan.Ph.d Dissertation, Harvard University.Cambridg,Massachusett. University Microfilm International.Ann Arbor

Cramb, Alan
2005   A Short history of Metals. Department of Metal Science and Engineering. Carnegie Mellon University (http://neon.mems. cmu.edu, accessed on 2005.09.15).

Dizon, Eusebio Z.
1983   The Metal Age in the Philippines: An Archaeometallurgical Investigation. Anthropological Papers No. 12, National Museum, Manila.

Dizon, Eusebio Z.
1988   Iron Age in the Philippines? A Critical Examination. Ph.d Dissertation.University of Pennsylvannia. University Microfilm International. Ann Arbor.

Dizon, Eusebio Z.
1990   "Prehistoric Iron and Its Technology". National Museum Papers Volume 1, No.1.

Feirer, John L.
1983   *General Metals*. 3rd ed. New York: McGraw-Hill.
Fenner, Bruce
1985   Cebu Under the Spanish Flag, 1521–1896: An Economic and Social History. University of San Carlos Publications, Cebu.

Foronda, Joseph V.
1994   Sequence Stratigraphy of an Oligocene-Miocene mixed Silic-lastic Carbonate System, Visayan Basin, Central Philippines, Bonn.

Fox, Robert B. and Avelino Legaspi.
1977   *Excavation at Santa Ana*. Manila: National Museum of the Philippines,

Gove, Philip B. and Merriam-Webster Editorial Staff
1981   Webster's Third New International Dictionary of English Language Unabridged Massachussett: Meriam-Webster Inc.

Hohl, Rudolf (ed.)
1987   Die Entwicklungsgeschichte der Erde, 5th ed. Dausien: Hanau.

Hutterer, Karl L.
1973   An Archaeological Picture of a Pre-Spanish Cebuano Community. Cebu City: San Carlos Publications.

Hutterer, Karl L. and William K. Macdonald, (eds).
1982   Houses Build on Scattered Poles: Prehistory and Ecology in Negros Oriental, Philippines. Cebu City: San Carlos University Press.

Junker, Laura L.
1989   "The Organization of Intra-Regional and Long Distance Trade in Pre-hispanic Philippine Complex Societies" Paper presented at the Society for American Archaeology Meetings. Atlanta, Georgia, 5–9 April.

Kobak, Cantius, J. OFM
1969   "Alzina's Historia de las Islas e Indios de Bisayas... 1668" Leyte-Samar Studies. Vol. III, No. 1.

Longacre, William
1981   "Kalinga Pottery: An Ethnographic Study," *Past Studies in Honor of David Clarke*. I. Hodder, G. Isaac & N. Hammond (eds.), Cambridge

Nishimura, Masao
1988   "Long Distance Trade and the Development of Complex Societies in the Prehistory of Central Philippines – The Cebu Archaeological Project: Basic Concept and First Results." Philippine Quarterly of Culture & Society. Vol. 16: 107–157.

Nolledo, Jose N. (editor)
1989   The Civil Code of the Philippines. Manila: National Bookstore, Inc.

Maceda, Marcelino
1991   "Preliminary Report on Selected Archaeological Sites in Southern Leyte: A Case for Salvage Archaeology". University Journal Vol. 3: 53–73.

Mascuñana, Rolando. V.
1989   "Blacksmiths and Gaffs in Dumaguete." Philippine Quarterly of Culture & Society, Vol. 17: 175–201.

Miksic, John
1995   Evolving Archaeological Perspectives on Southeast Asian. Journal of Southeast Asian Studies. Vol. 26(1): 46-62.

Miller, Elmer S. and Weitz, Charles A.
1979   Introduction to Anthropology Englewood Cliffs, New Jersey, Prentice-Hall, Inc. p. 470.

Momongan, Perla C.
1992   Mineral Resources of the Province of Cebu and its Industrial Uses. DENR, Mines and Geosciences Development Service. (Typscript)

Mudar, Karen and Torre, Amalia (de la)
1986   "The Becino Site: An Exercise in Ethnoarchaeology." K. Hutterer and W. Macdonald (eds.) *Houses Built on Scattered Poles: Prehistory and Ecology in Negros Oriental, Philippines.* University of San Carlos, Cebu City, pp. 117–146.

Orme, Bryony
1974   "Twentieth-Century Prehistorians and the Idea of Ethnographic Parallels." *MAN* (N.S.) 9.

Porth, Hans, Carla Müller and Curt von Daniels
1989   The Sedimentary Formations of the Visayas Basin, Philippines. Band 70. pp 29–87.

Russ, John C.
1976   Principles of EDAX Analysis on the Electron Microscope: Lecture and Workshop Notes, EDAX International, Inc.

Scott, William Henry.
1985   Cracks in the Parchment Curtain and Other Essays in Philippine History. Quezon City.

Sinopoli, Carla M.
1991   "Seeking the Past through the Present: Recent Ethno-archaeological Research in Southeast Asia" *Asian Perspectives*, Vol 30 (2): 177–192.

Solheim, Wilhelm G.
1964   The Archaeology of Central Philippines: A Study Chiefly of Iron Age and its Relationships. Bureau of Printing Manila.

Tan, Leonidas
1969   "The Economics of Blacksmithing Industry in Basak, Cebu City" (Cebu City: unpublished Master Thesis, University of San Carlos).

Tenazas, Rosa.
1968   A Report on the Archaeology of the Locsin-University of San Carlos Excavations in Pila, Laguna. n.p.: September 4, 1967 – March 19, 1968.

Tenazas, Rosa.
1973   "The Salvage Excavation of Southern Luzon Philippines: A Summary." *Philippine Quarterly of Culture & Society*. Vol. 1, 132–136.

Torre, Amalia de la and N. Tubalado-Cuevas
1990   "A Preliminary Investigation of a Blacksmith's Workshop in Barangay Basak-Pardo, Cebu City" (Manila: Archaeology Record Section, National Museum of the Philippines. (Typescript)

Ziegert, Helmut
1980   "Objektorientierte und Problemorientierte Forschungsansätze in der Archäologie". Hephaistos: Kritische Zeitschrift zur Theorie und Praxis der Archäologie und angrenzender Wissenschaften. Band 2.

Ziegert, Helmut
1992   Drochtersen-Ritsch: Zur frühgeschichichlichen Besiedlung in Südkehdingen. – Beiträge des Landkeises Stade zur regionalen Themen. Band 9. Landkreis Stade. Stade.

"Der Aktualistische Vergleich als Grundlage archäologisch-historischer Interpretation. In: Ethnographisch-archäologische Zeitschrift (EAZ), Bd 35, Berlin 1994 (1995), 177–198.

2002   Archaeology as History. A Track in the Past. Hamburg 2002. BOD (Books on Demand).